William Hurrell Mallock

Classes and Masses

Or, Wealth, Wages, and Welfare in the United Kingdom

William Hurrell Mallock

Classes and Masses
Or, Wealth, Wages, and Welfare in the United Kingdom

ISBN/EAN: 9783337143510

Printed in Europe, USA, Canada, Australia, Japan

Cover: Foto ©ninafisch / pixelio.de

More available books at **www.hansebooks.com**

CLASSES AND MASSES

OR

WEALTH, WAGES, AND WELFARE IN
THE UNITED KINGDOM

A HANDBOOK OF SOCIAL FACTS FOR POLITICAL
THINKERS AND SPEAKERS

BY

W. H. MALLOCK

LONDON
ADAM AND CHARLES BLACK
1896

PREFACE

THE present volume, the substance of which, together with the illustrations, originally appeared at intervals in the *Pall Mall Magazine*, is addressed to practical people, who realise how closely social problems are now connected with political; and it is addressed especially to people who are engaged in political work and speaking. Such people know how easily questions arising from the economic condition of the masses may endanger the popularity of a government in times otherwise tranquil; and desire, but are often unable, when such a question confronts them, to bring to its consideration some distinct, if general, knowledge of the main facts underlying it, and the principles fundamentally involved. Now these questions take very various forms, each of which is complicated by its own special details; but in all of them are involved certain common facts and principles, which are comparatively few and simple, and with regard to which certain definite information can be given. The present volume is an attempt to deal with the most important of these last in a way so simple as to render them intelligible to everybody, and to enable any one, without any previous training, to discuss them with confidence on a public platform, and apply them to the arguments and demands of agitators and excitable reformers.

The facts and principles to which allusion is now made are divisible into two groups, which may be described as follows. Whenever any demand is made for legislative interference with the existing organisation of society, and the natural working of the economic forces embodied in it, such demands are nearly always accompanied by, and indeed are logically based upon, a wholesale indictment of society as it now exists; and the counts in this indictment are familiar enough to all of us. Society, as now organised, is said to be essentially unjust. It is said that its natural, and indeed its necessary, tendency is to confine the benefits of progress more and more strictly to the few, and to push down the masses of the people into ever-deepening poverty and servitude, rendering their chances of making even a bare living more and more uncertain. Hence, it is argued, arises the obvious necessity of arbitrarily interfering by law with existing social institutions. There has been hardly a single social agitator, during the past twenty years in England, who has not put forward the above statements with regard to society as obvious and incontrovertible truths. It is therefore, before all things, necessary to inquire how far such a hideous picture is correct; and of the two groups of facts and principles with which this volume deals, one has reference to the character of society as it is—to the natural tendency of the forces embodied in it, and the actual results of their working, as shown by an examination of the general condition of the people at the present moment, and a comparison of it with their condition at former periods. The conclusions to which such an inquiry and comparison lead are in the highest degree striking, and are absolutely unequivocal; and it is essential to every political speaker that he should be familiar with them. They comprise an answer, complete at every point, to the dangerous commonplaces of the agitator; and the first and last portions of this volume deal with them.

The facts and principles comprised in the other group have reference not to the natural working of the economic forces that at present exist, but to the manner and extent to which it is proposed to interfere with them. The principal object of such proposed interference is nearly always the same, namely, an increase, by means of legislation, in the wages of the mass of the people generally, or of some particular section of them; and at the bottom of all such proposals there is always to be found one or other of two theories, and sometimes both. One of these theories is, that it is possible to raise the condition of the people as a whole by establishing a minimum wage, sufficient to maintain a man in some given degree of decency and comfort, and prohibiting employers from ever paying less than this. The other is the theory that any standard of living assumed to be reasonable for the wage earners in any given industry, can be made to regulate the prices at which the proceeds of that industry are sold, so as to secure wages for the men by which this standard of living may be maintained. These two theories form the subject of the remainder of this volume. Each is reduced to its simplest elements, and is exhibited in connection with facts and principles which are common to all economic life, and which would affect the earnings of the various classes of workers, and the minimum standard of living, as much in a socialistic state as they would in any other. No attempt is made to urge any detailed conclusions on the reader. All that is done is to put before him certain elementary truths on which any sane conclusions must be based, with regard to each special case as it arises.

In order to render the information and the arguments conveyed in the following pages as clear and intelligible as possible to the ordinary reader and the ordinary practical man, the statistics and the arguments are alike illustrated by diagrams and pictures. The latter are used as a species of working model, to show the operation of those natural conditions and universal principles of action by which the distribution of wealth and the amount of men's earnings are regulated in every state of society. The former—that is to say the diagrams as distinguished from the pictures—are used to convey to the eye, at a single glance, the significance of the statistical figures.

As was said just now, these figures, which show us the actual results and tendencies of society as at present organised, constitute the kind of information with which it is most important that the political speaker should familiarise himself; and accordingly the first question dealt with will be the question of how wealth is distributing itself at the present moment, and what is the natural effect of modern industrial progress on the financial condition of the working classes, or, in other words, on the great majority of the nation.

February 1896.

CONTENTS

CHAPTER I

HOW IS WEALTH DISTRIBUTING ITSELF

	PAGE
The ordinary generalisation of the Socialist, and the Emotional Reformer, that the Rich are getting richer, the Poor poorer, the Middle Class disappearing—this is the exact opposite of the Truth	1
The Sole Fact that makes it plausible—the existence of a certain Residuum. Its approximate Numbers at the present day	3
Its absolute Increase, but its relative Diminution	4
Pauperism in the years 1850 and 1882. Pauperism at Sheffield in the year 1615	4
The actual and relative Cost of Pauperism from 1700 to 1880 (illustrated by a diagram)	5
The Residuum not the Result of the existing System. It is rather an Element which has failed to be absorbed by it	6
The tendency of the existing System, as shown in nine-tenths of the Population, is to make the Poor richer, the Rich slightly poorer, and to augment the Middle Classes	7
Precise meaning given here to the words, "Rich," "Poor," and "Middle Classes"	8
"The Working Classes" used to include all with Incomes under £150	10
Growth of the National Income since the year 1775—its actual Growth, and Growth relative to the Population (illustrated by diagram on page 12)	11
Relative Increase of the "Working Classes" and the classes that pay Income-tax, between the years 1850 and 1880 (with diagram)	14

	PAGE
Increase in the Numbers and Increase of various sections of the Middle Classes and the Rich (with diagram on page 15)	16
The Middle Classes, instead of being crushed out, are the Classes that have increased fastest. (Diagram on page 19)	18
The small body of Millionaires—exceptional Facts relating to them	19
The Rich increasing more slowly than the Middle Classes, and becoming individually slightly poorer, whilst the Middle Classes are becoming individually slightly richer. (Diagram on page 22)	20
Aggregate Incomes of the Millionaires, the very Rich, and the Middle Classes, as compared with the entire National Income. (Diagram on page 24)	23
The Working Classes. Their growth in Wealth far greater than that of even the Middle Classes	25
The Extent of this astonishing Growth not generally realised	26
The Working Classes richer per head at the present day than their Fathers would have been thirty years ago had the whole National Wealth been divided between them. Statistics (and diagram on page 26)	28
Explanation of the sketch at the head of this chapter	31
Proportion of the Working Classes receiving Wages of various amounts. (Diagram, page 32)	31
The Residuum represents not general Economic Tendencies, but an exception to them	32

CHAPTER II

THE MINIMUM OF HUMANE LIVING

The doctrine of a "Living Wage" true within certain limits	34
The idea of a "Minimum Standard" being accepted, how is this standard to be determined?	35
The great Coal-Strike and the Minimum Standard	36
Vague ideas as to what the Minimum Standard, as a General Standard, is	38
Sentimental Misconception of the typical Human Lot	39

	PAGE
A Minimum Standard of Living, though adopted by Sentiment as a Principle, is necessarily limited, practically, by external Facts—	41
And firstly, by the Amount of the National Income at the time	41
It would therefore differ greatly in various countries. (Diagram, page 43)	42
The practical limit of the Minimum Standard, supplied by the Income made by the Cultivator of the Worst Soil allowed to be cultivated	45
Detailed Explanation of this Statement	47
The Maximum Income of the poorest class of Cultivators cannot be more than the value of their total Produce	48
Qualities of Land in the United Kingdom. Amount of Land of each Quality (with diagram on page 50)	49
Unequal position of Equal Men on Unequal Soils (with diagram)	51
The same Fact illustrated more fully (with diagram, page 53)	52
So long as we acquiesce in the poorest Soils being cultivated at all, their total Produce must form the limit of our Minimum Standard of Living	54
Though this may be raised, and has been raised with the progress of the Arts, etc., and is modified by the circumstances of different Industries	60

CHAPTER III

WAGES AND THE PRODUCTS OF WORK

The above conclusion connected with a wider one	62
Recapitulation of preceding argument (with diagram)	63
Remission of all Rent to the Cultivators of poorest Soils would hardly affect the question of Rent on superior Soils, either in principle or practice (with diagram)	64
The subject of the Minimum Standard, or Income of the poorest Cultivator, resumed	67
Analysis of his Income. The larger part consists not of what he produces himself, but of what he gets in exchange for his products	68

	PAGE
This Fact illustrated by a Community of three Men (with diagram on pages 68 and 70).	69
The Bread Producer, the Clothes Producer, and the Maker of Furniture	71
How the Income of each consists mainly of the Products of the other (with diagram on page 70)	72
Analysis of what must happen if these Incomes increase (with diagram on page 72)	73
The Increment in the case of each Producer depends on what *others* will give him for his products	75
This is equally true whether "the Producer" is the individual wage-earner, or a body consisting of wage-earners and a Capitalist or Landlord (with diagram on pages 74 and 75).	76
We may therefore treat Wages as if the entire value of the entire Product of each industry was divided equally amongst the Workmen.	77
The Workman's Income depends on what the rest of the Community can be induced to give him for what he produces	78
The Strike Leaders in the great Coal-Strike tried to persuade the Colliers that what the Community would give depended on what the Colliers wanted	79
The case of Coal Supply, as regards the Community, examined (with diagram).	80
Wages *must* follow prices	81
Except in the case of absolute necessaries, when produced by monopolists	83
This Truth illustrated by referring again to the imaginary Community already dealt with (with diagram)	84
The Wages of the Maker of Superfluities must follow prices	90
Application of this Analysis to the demands of the British Colliers. (Diagrams, page 93)	92
As Civilisation advances, Wages depend more and more completely on the Consumers, or the price they will consent to pay	95

CHAPTER IV

THE CENSUS AND THE CONDITION OF THE PEOPLE

	PAGE
The actual Condition of the People of the United Kingdom, as illustrated by a variety of salient Facts	98
The Capital Value of the Country, and the elements that constitute its Capital (with diagram on page 101)	99
Money, Land, Houses, Furniture, Public Works, Gas and Water Works, Railways, etc.	102
The Income that comes into this Country from Investments in other Countries	103
Special significance of this Income in argument with Socialistic Agitators	104
The Population—the large proportion of it that is composed of Children; the small proportion that is composed of adult Males (with diagram, page 105)	104
Married Persons, Bachelors, and Spinsters (with diagram, page 107)	106
The Proportion of the Population that lives at leisure on independent Incomes	108
The extremely small number of this Class	110
Were its members made to work the general result would be inappreciable	111
The Housing of the Population	111
The number of Families in England and Wales housed respectively in dwellings of one room, two rooms, three rooms, four rooms, and more than four rooms (with diagram, page 113)	112
The tendency of the Changes that are taking place in this respect illustrated by the history of Scotland during the past ten years (with diagram, page 115)	114
The natural Economic Tendencies of the times, illustrated by the Increase and Decrease of various callings and industries (with diagram on page 119)	117
Clergy of the Established Church	117
Nonconformist Clergy	117
Roman Catholic Clergy	117
Agriculturers, Farmers, Market Gardeners	118
The Cotton Industry, Domestic Servants	118

	PAGE
School Teachers, Commercial Travellers, Shopkeepers, Clerks	120
Small Businesses not being crushed out	121
Growth of the Classes that minister to the wellbeing of the Poor	121
Enormous Increase in the Business of the Post-office Savings Banks	122
Relative Strength of the Establishment and other Religious Bodies (with diagram on page 124)	123
The Productivity of Agriculture, as related to Land Systems. A Comparison between certain Agricultural Facts in various Countries (with diagram on page 129)	125
The Housing of the Poor: the Reasons for its Deficiency	129
Not due on the whole to the Extortion of Ground Landlords	129
The Actual Rental of the United Kingdom, urban and rural	130
Grotesque and ignorant Exaggeration of Radical Agitators	130
Methods of arriving at the Total	131
The Ground Rental of London, as distinct from the Total Rental	132
The Rental of the Country, as generally stated in Radical Publications, has no relation to truth whatsoever	134
The varying degrees of Overcrowding in the Principal Towns in England (with diagram on page 135)	134
Rental is obviously not the Determining Factor	136
The Facts of the case full of hope for the moderate Reformer	138
Concluding observations	138

CHAPTER I

HOW IS WEALTH DISTRIBUTING ITSELF?

THE general tendency of our modern conditions of industry, so far as concerns the distribution of wealth generally, was, up to a very recent period, altogether misunderstood; and in many quarters it is so still. It was, and by multitudes of people it still is, believed to be the exact reverse of what events and investigations show it to be. The celebrated Socialist writer, Karl Marx, not thirty years ago, laid it down as an incontrovertible fact that under our existing industrial system three things were happening:

that the majority of the community were constantly getting poorer; that moderate fortunes were steadily disappearing; and that all wealth, beyond the bare means of living, was steadily passing into fewer and fewer hands, so that the ultimate result would be sooner or later this—a nation of slaves living on starvation wages on the one side, and a few "great capitalist lords," as Marx called them, on the other. This view of the case, fraught as it was and as Marx meant it to be, with promise or menace of some vast social catastrophe, has been not only adopted by his own Socialistic followers, and used by them as a text in all their popular preaching, but has also been put forward as the result of independent observation by sentimentalists, philanthropists, and reformers of all kinds, —Carlyle, for instance, may be mentioned amongst the number,—and it has embodied itself in a saying which has become almost proverbial: that the rich are getting richer, and the poor poorer, and thus the middle classes are being crushed out. My aim in the present paper is to show as clearly as possible the entire fallacy of this view;

but first it will be well to direct the reader's attention to a fact which makes it plausible, and accounts for its origin and persistence.

Speaking in round numbers, there exists in this country to-day a population consisting of about 700,000 families, or 3,000,000 persons, whose means of subsistence are either insufficient, or barely sufficient, or precarious, and the conditions of whose life generally are either hard or degrading, or both. A large portion of them may, without any sentimental exaggeration, be called miserable, and all of them may be called unfortunate. There is, further, this observation to be made. People who are in want of the bare necessaries of life can hardly be worse off absolutely at one period than another; but if, whilst their own poverty remains the same, the riches of other classes increase, they do, in a certain sense, become worse off relatively. The statement, therefore, that the poor are getting constantly poorer, is, in this relative sense, true of a certain part of the population; and that part is now nearly equal in numbers to the entire population of the country at the time of the

Norman Conquest. Such being the case, it is of course obvious that persons who, for purposes of either benevolence or agitation, are concerned to discover want, misfortune, and misery, find it easier to do so now than at any former period. But this view of the question, though true so far as it goes, is, if taken by itself, altogether misleading, and points to conclusions the exact reverse of the truth. This unfortunate class, though it has increased in numbers absolutely, has grown less and less numerous relatively to the entire population; and the periods during which its absolute growth has been most rapid have been the periods during which its relative decrease has been most rapid also. In illustration of this fact it may be mentioned that, whereas in 1850 there were 9 paupers to every 200 inhabitants, in 1882 there were only 5; whilst, to turn for a moment to a far more distant time, so as to compare the new industrial system with the old, in the year 1615 a survey of Sheffield, already a manufacturing centre, showed that the "begging poor," who "could not live without the charity of their neighbours," actually amounted to one-third of the population, or 725 households out of 2207. Further, although, as I observed just now, it is in a certain sense true to say that, relatively to other classes the unfortunate class has been getting poorer, the real tendency of events is expressed in a much truer way by saying that all other classes have

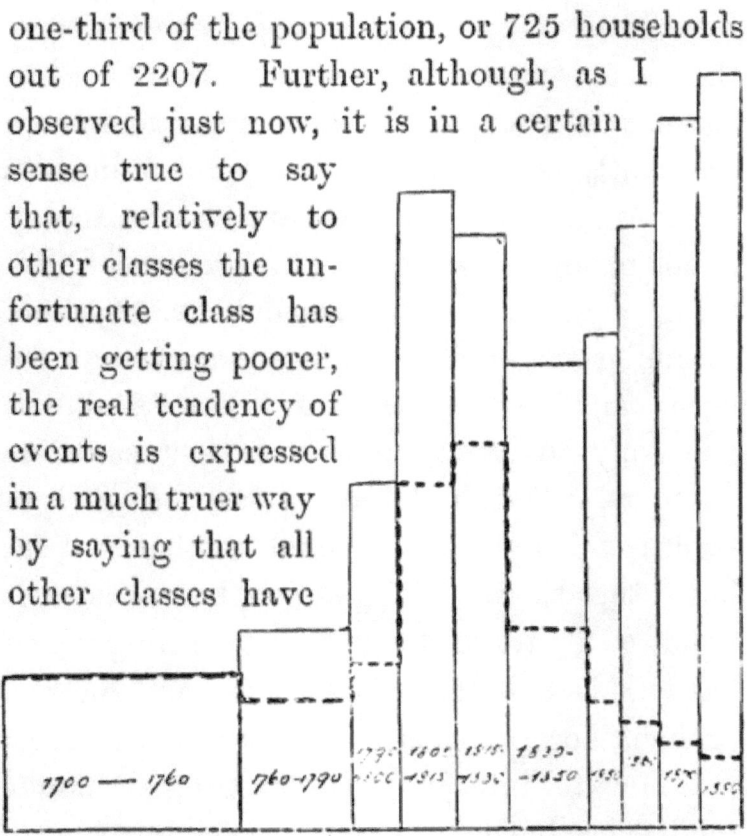

Fig. 1.

The Actual and Relative cost of Pauperism for 180 Years.

The entire columns represent the actual amounts spent; the dotted line represents the increase or decrease of these amounts relative to the national income.

been getting more and more removed from poverty. That the existence of the unfortunate class is at once dangerous and deplorable is not to be denied. From certain points of view, and for certain purposes, it is impossible to treat the fact too gravely or too earnestly; but those who most fully realise its gravity are constantly betrayed into misapprehending its significance. The unfortunate class of to-day is not in any sense a sign or product of anything special in our modern industrial system. A similar class existed before that system was born; and that system, as I have said, has relatively reduced and not increased its numbers. The right way, indeed, in which to regard it is, not as a product of that system, but rather as something which has resisted it —not as a part of it, but as something which has failed to be absorbed by it; and the real problem for philanthropists and reformers is, not how to interfere with existing economic tendencies, but how, so far as possible, to bring the residuum under their influence. In considering, therefore, what these economic tendencies are, we must put the unfortunate class altogether on one side: that is to say, out of the 37,000,000 inhabitants of this country we must put aside the exceptional case of 3,000,000, and confine our attention to the representative case of 34,000,000.

If we do this we shall find that the saying which I began with quoting, namely, that the rich are getting richer, the poor are getting poorer, and the middle classes are being crushed out, is not only a not true statement of facts, but is in every word an absolute and exact inversion of them. We shall find that the poor are getting richer, the rich, on an average, getting poorer, and that of all classes in the community the middle class is growing the fastest.

There is a popular, but very misleading saying, to the effect that statistics can be made to prove anything. This is true only if the figures are false, or if the facts or things referred to are not clearly defined. Actual falsification of figures is not perhaps a common offence; and those which I shall give presently are taken from the most authoritative sources. But figures which are accurate in themselves can be made altogether untrustworthy if the facts or things they refer to are described in ambiguous language. Socialist writers, for instance, are constantly issuing leaflets, in which it is declared that "the workers," "the producers," or "the labourers," get less than a quarter of the total national income, whilst the idle classes, who live on them, get more than three-quarters of it. The figures these persons quote are not their own invention; but what is their own invention is their definition of the word "producers"—a definition which they carefully abstain from giving, but which, if their figures have any foundation in fact, is obviously inconsistent with all ordinary usage, and is contradicted by most of their own reasoning. In order, therefore, that the reader may know exactly what I am talking about, and give their right significance to the figures I am about to quote, let me state the precise meaning which I shall attach to three important terms—"the working classes," "the middle classes," and "the rich." By the "working classes" I mean that portion of the population which does not pay income-tax, and which consists of individuals and families with less than £150 a year. By "the middle classes," which I shall divide into two sections, I mean individuals or families with incomes ranging from £150 to £1000; and by "the rich," whom I shall divide into different sections also, I mean individuals or families with incomes above £1000. It is hardly necessary to observe that, for purposes like the present, our classification of the rich and the middle classes is altogether financial, and that the term "middle classes" is used without any of its social meanings; but it will be perhaps desirable to say a few words in defence of the application of the term "working classes" to all individuals or families with less than £150 a year. These classes, no doubt, include a considerable number of persons who are not manual labourers; though when we come to consider that, according to the latest evidence, the artisans who earn very nearly £150 amount to at least 180,000, and that in certain industries many of them earn more, it will be seen that the income-tax test is more accurate than might be supposed. At all events, whether the classes in question are manual labourers or not, they are, with very unimportant exceptions, wage-earners, that is to say, for whatever money they receive they give work which is estimated at at least the same money value. A schoolmaster, for instance, who receives £150 a year gives in return teaching which is valued at the same sum.

School-teaching is wealth just as much as a school-house; it figures in all estimates as part of the income of the nation; and therefore the schoolmaster is a producer just as much as the school-builder. The classes, then, with incomes of less than £150 are, as a whole, producers in this sense of the word, that whenever a sum of money is paid to them, a corresponding sum is estimated as being added to the general wealth; and it is thus substantially accurate to speak of them as the "working classes." Anyhow, whether the reader approve of the term or not, he knows the sense in which I am using it; and that is the essential thing.

Let us now proceed to facts. Before we inquire how the modern industrial system has affected the distribution of wealth, we must obtain a clear idea of how it has affected the production of it. Ordinary people are entirely unaware of what the growth of wealth in this country during the past hundred years has been. They are aware, in a vague way, that the country has grown richer; but much of this growth they attribute to the growth of population; and, as I observed just now, many of them vaguely believe that, relatively to the population, the country has grown poorer. The real state of the case is exhibited in Fig. 2, on the next page, which will show the reader more at a single glance than he could probably gather from whole pages of explanation. The shortest column represents the income of the country as it was in the year 1775; the taller columns, which have dates attached to them, represent its growth from that time to the present. The lower and lighter portion represents what the growth of wealth would have been had the productive power of industry undergone no development, and had wealth grown only on account of, and in proportion to, the growth of the population. The upper and darker portion represents the growth of wealth which has been due entirely to machinery, science, and organisation; and both portions together represent the actual growth in its entirety. The lower portion, besides representing the growth of wealth accounted for by the growth of population, will, as is obvious, represent the growth of population also.

Here, then, in their broad outlines, are the facts whose details and whose social meaning we have to examine and analyse. We see what this astonishing growth of wealth has been. We must next see how, and amongst what classes, it has been distributed. Our survey of the growth of the national income as a whole extended some way back into the last century; but we shall find ourselves obliged, in considering its distribution, to confine our attention to more limited periods, according to the fulness of the information accessible as to the various points involved. I will deal first with the case of the

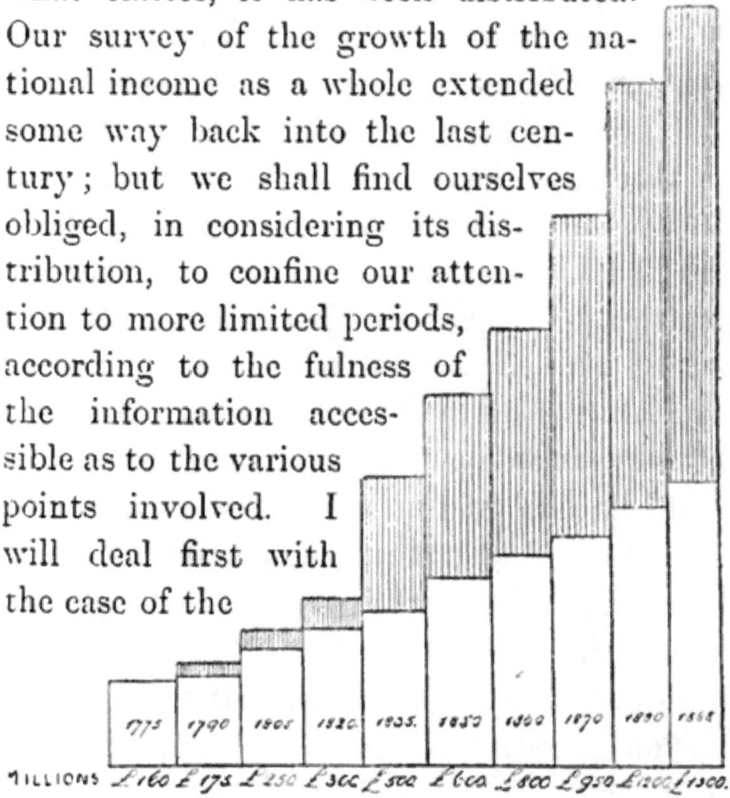

MILLIONS £160 £175 £250 £300 £500 £600 £800 £950 £1100 £1300.

1775 1790 1805 1820 1835 1850 1860 1870 1880 1888

Fig. 2.

rich and the middle classes, showing how the growth of wealth has affected them, and with degree of truth it can be said that the former are growing richer and the latter being crushed out. Professor Leone Levi, about ten years ago, treated this subject, within limits, in a most exhaustive way. His inquiries did not extend farther back than 1850; but the period which he covered happened to be the period when the modern industrial system was reaching its fullest development, and when the social changes produced by it were becoming most rapid and remarkable. I shall therefore confine myself to giving, in a simple and intelligible form, the results which were arrived at by this eminent statistician, but which, owing to the form in which they were stated by him, have failed hitherto to reach the popular ear, and have certainly never been grasped by the imagination of practical politicians.

In the first place, we must realise the broad fact that, rapid as has been the increase of the population as a whole, the increase of the classes that pay income-tax has been far more rapid. During the period of which I am speaking the population, as a whole, increased from 27,000,000 to 35,000,000; the section of the population living on incomes that paid income-tax increased from

1,500,000 to 4,700,000. Thus, if the increase of the whole was in the proportion of 27 to 35, the increase of the section in question was in the proportion of 27 to 84. The difference between the two rates of increase is illustrated in Fig. 3. It is essential to bear the above fact in mind, because it shows that the growth in wealth of the rich and the middle

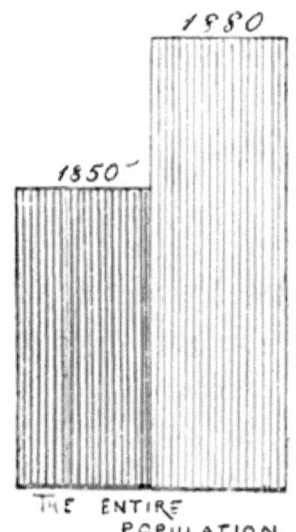

Fig. 3.

classes does not mean the growth of fortunes

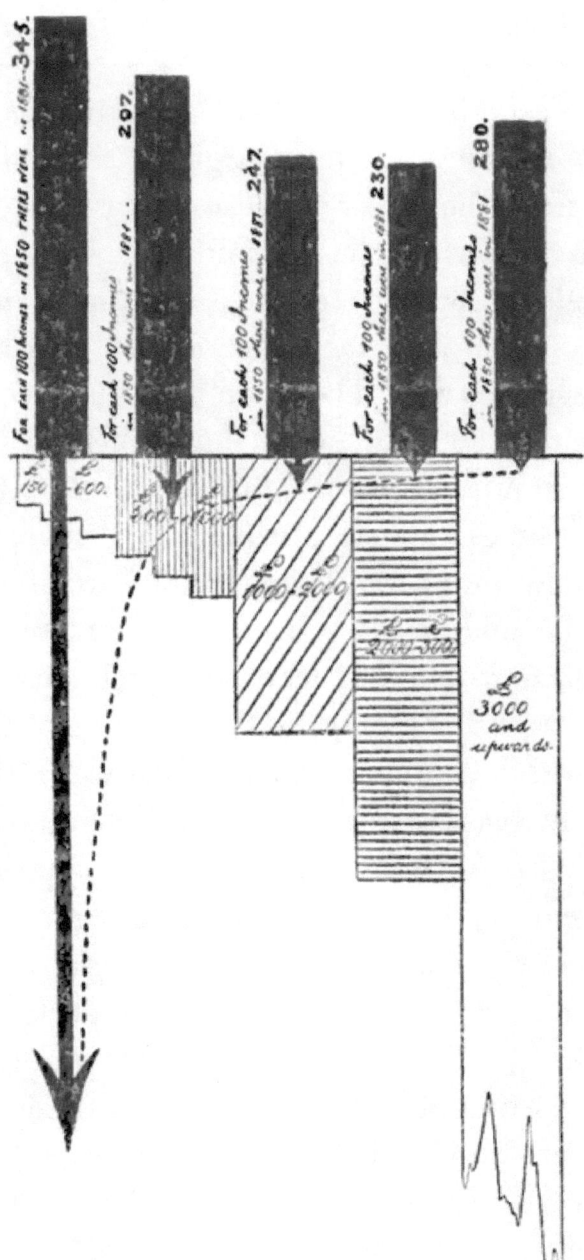

Fig. 4.

already established, but the constant creation of new fortunes, small or large, by individuals rising from the ranks of the working classes.

Let us now divide the middle classes from the rich, according to the definition I have already given, and see which of the two have increased most. The number of incomes between £150 and £1000 have increased (in round numbers) from 300,000 to 990,000. The incomes above £1000 have increased (in round numbers) from 24,000 to 60,000. Thus the middle class has been increased by 690,000 new families, whilst the rich class has been increased by only 36,000. But not only is there this enormous disparity between their actual increase: there is a considerable disparity also between their relative increase; and again it is the middle class which has increased the more largely. The middle class has increased numerically in the proportion of 3 to 10; the rich class has increased only in the proportion of 3 to 8. In Fig. 4 these two classes are subdivided: the middle class into persons with incomes between £150 and £600, and persons with incomes between £600 and £1000; and the rich are subdivided into persons with incomes between £1000 and £2000, persons with incomes between £2000 and £3000, and persons with incomes of £3000 and upwards. The lower columns in the diagram represent the relative magnitudes of the various incomes dealt with. The black columns represent the proportion in which the number of persons enjoying each class of income in the year 1850 increased between that year and the year 1881; and the arrows pointing downwards represent the actual number of new incomes added in each case. The reader is thus able to see at a glance how grotesque is the fallacy that represents the middle classes as being crushed out. He will see that, in absolute contradiction to the popular view, the middle classes are increasing with far greater rapidity than the rich—in fact, that their increase is the most distinctive and extraordinary feature of the time; whilst, if we compare their increase with that of the working classes, it becomes more startling and more extraordinary still. Fig. 5 will help the reader to realise this. The total population increased from about 27,500,000 to 35,000,000; whilst the income-tax-paying population was, as has been said already, 1,500,000 in 1850, and more than 4,500,000 in 1881. If, then, we deduct these two amounts from the totals at the two dates, we have a working class population of 26,000,000 in 1850, and of 30,500,000 in 1881. The working classes have increased, therefore, by about 15 per cent, whilst the middle classes had increased by more than 300 per cent.

The only facts that seem, even for a moment, to coincide, however loosely, with the popular view, are as follows:—First, there is the fact that the increase per cent of the classes with incomes of more than £3000 a year has been greater than that of the classes with incomes between that amount and £1000. The actual increase, however, of the former is more than three times as great as the actual increase of the latter—that of the former being 27,000, and that of the latter 9000, whilst the total numbers in 1881 were respectively 45,000 and 15,000.[1] And, however

---

[1] According to the facts compiled by Professor Leone Levi, aided by information given by Mr. Gripper of the Inland Revenue, there were in the year 1881 about 15,000 incomes in the United Kingdom

HOW IS WEALTH DISTRIBUTING ITSELF? 19

the different sections of the rich class may compare with one another in point of growth, even the smallest section, which has grown the fastest, has been entirely distanced by the yet faster growth of the middle class. There remains, however, another set of facts to be mentioned. If we subdivide the rich class yet farther, we shall find that there is one section which has not only increased in numbers, but whose members have grown richer as individuals. This is the richest class—the class composed of persons with £50,000 a year and over. In 1850 the average income of such persons was about £72,000; in

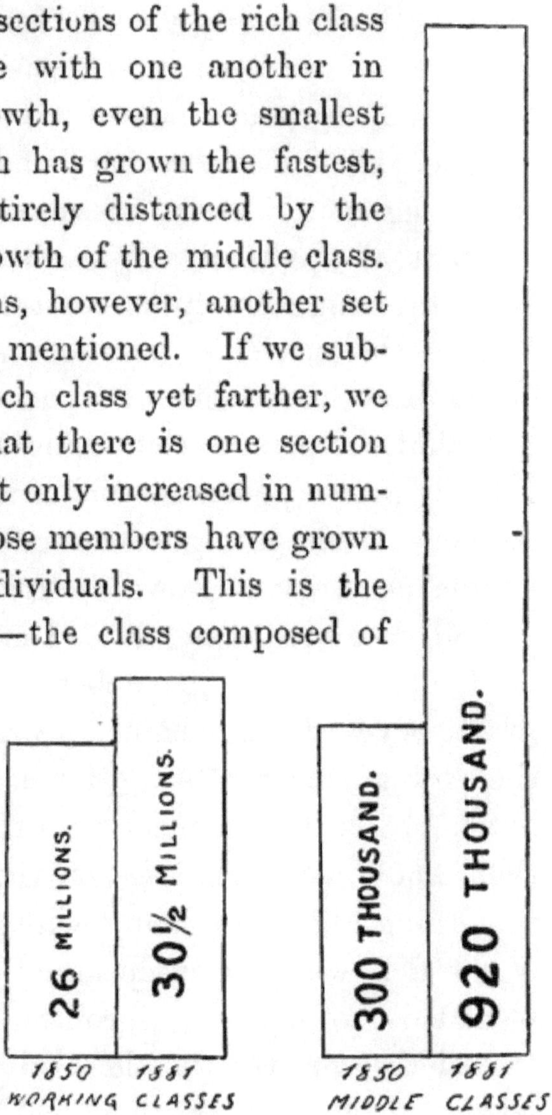

26 MILLIONS. | 30½ MILLIONS.
1850 | 1881
WORKING CLASSES

300 THOUSAND. | 920 THOUSAND.
1850 | 1881
MIDDLE CLASSES

FIG. 5.

of over £3000 a year, 3000 of over £10,000 a year, and 230 of over £50,000.

1881 it was about £80,000. This class, however, is altogether exceptional. It consisted in 1881 of only 230 persons out of the 60,000 who had more than £1000 a year; and the amount of its aggregate income was not more than $4\frac{1}{2}$ per cent of the total assessed to income-tax. With the single exception of this handful of persons, the rich class has not only increased in numbers much more slowly than the middle class, but the persons composing it have individually grown poorer instead of richer; whilst the persons composing the larger section of the middle class have grown individually richer as well as more numerous. The incomes, indeed, of those who have between £600 and £1000 a year have remained nearly stationary, the average income being, for both 1850 and 1881, £735; but the incomes of those with less than £600 have increased on the average by something like 4 per cent; whilst the incomes of the rich, with the exception of 3000 persons —that is to say, the incomes of nineteen-twentieths of the whole body, possessing sixteen-twentieths of that body's aggregate wealth—have decreased on an average by very nearly 7 per cent. This is represented in

Fig. 6, p. 22. The sections of the column marked A, B, C, and D, represent the relative amounts of the aggregate incomes possessed by the various classes with which we are dealing. A represents the total of all incomes between £150 and £600; B the total of all incomes between £600 and £1000; C the total of all incomes between £1000 and £50,000; and D the total of all incomes of £50,000 and over. The lines rising to the points a and c represent the increase of the average individual incomes of the bulk of the middle class, and of the millionaires in 1881 as compared with 1850, whilst the lines sinking to the point b represent the average decrease of the individual incomes of the great body of the rich during the same period.

It will thus be seen that the small body of millionaires is the only class who, during the thirty years in question, justified the popular statement that the rich were growing richer; and, with regard to this class, there are three things to be said. Seventy-seven of the incomes comprised in it were derived from business; and with the growth of each of these business incomes at least as much

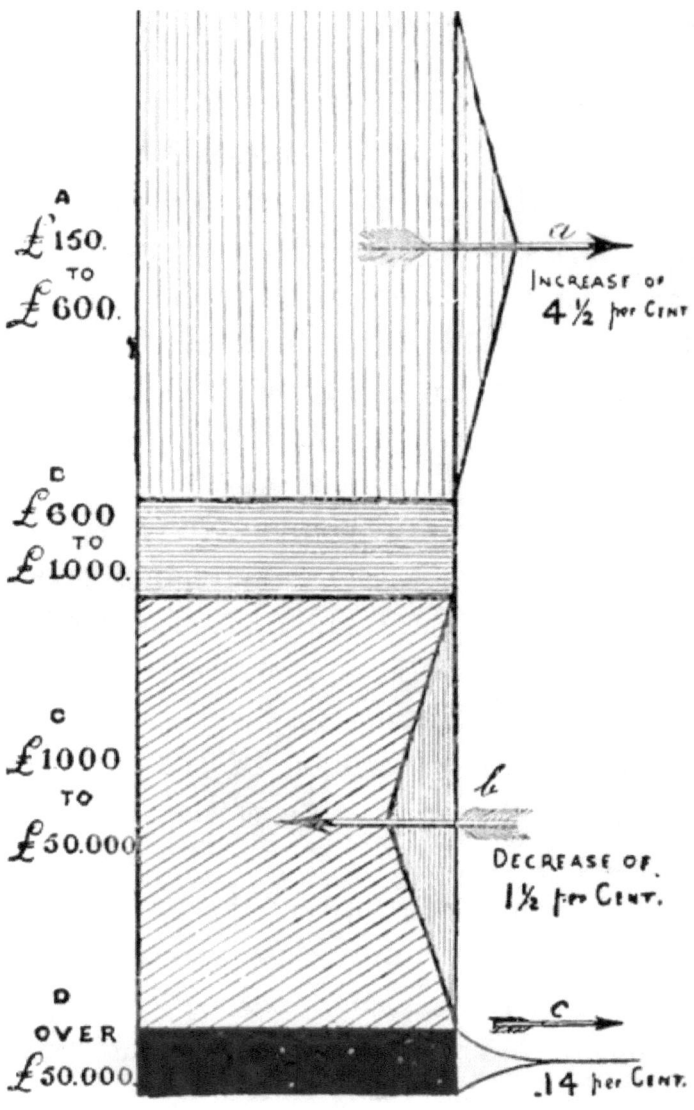

Fig. 6.

wealth was added to the nation at large as was taken by the recipient of the income. Sixty-six of such incomes were derived from land; and since 1880 these landed incomes have not increased, but decreased. They have decreased by 14 per cent in England, and by 13 per cent in Scotland; whilst, taking these great incomes as a whole, and comparing them with the wealth of the nation, their amount is so small that they might be merged in the general wealth, or altogether abstracted from it, without appreciably affecting the national wellbeing. The ordinary agitator delights to occupy himself with millionaires, and to represent their expenditure as some fatal drain on the resources of the community, or a gold mine from which a progressive income-tax might extract some colossal revenue. In Fig. 7, p. 24, the column marked A will illustrate how fallacious such ideas as these are. The three columns A, B, C, each represent the total national income, estimated at £1,300,000,000. In column A the minute black section at the top represents the total income of the millionaires—that is to say, £22,000,000 out of £1,300,000,000. This sum, if divided amongst

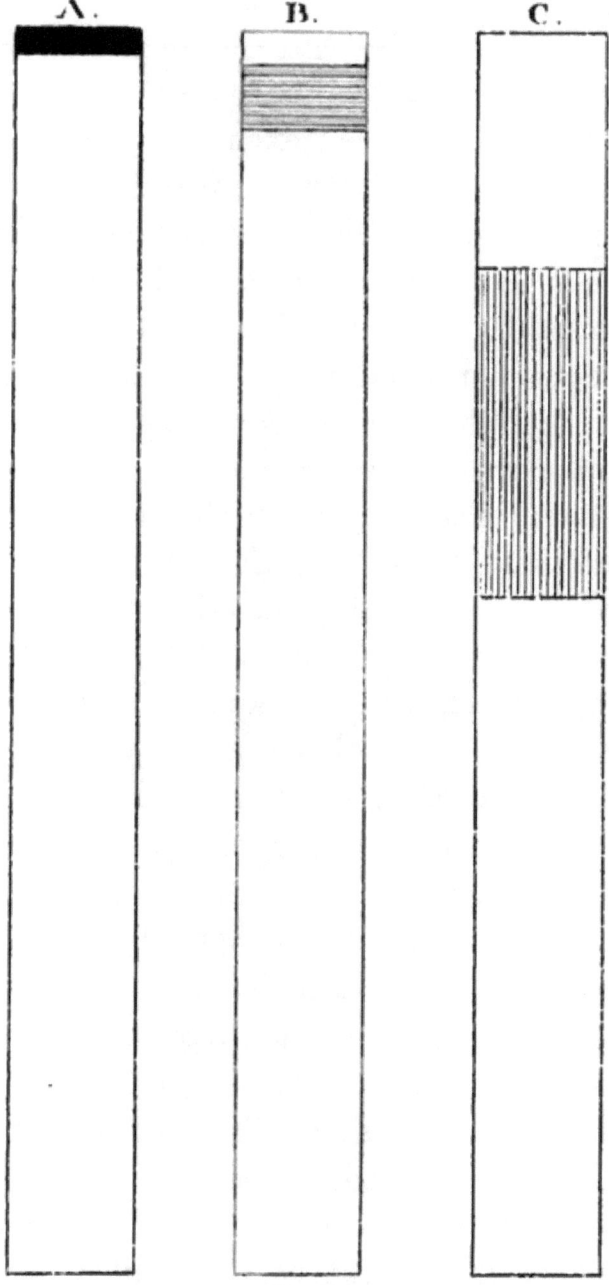

Fig. 7.

the population in equal shares, would yield each inhabitant a dividend of one shilling a month. In column B the shaded section represents the total incomes of all those persons whose incomes range from £5000 to £50,000; and the shaded section in column C represents the total income of the middle classes.

Let us now turn to the most important question of all—the condition of the working classes. It is impossible to imagine a more complete contradiction of the conventional view of the agitator than is offered by the facts of the case. Instead of getting poorer, instead of finding it harder to gain a living, the working classes have increased in wealth far faster than any other class in the community. They have not, indeed, increased in numbers so fast as the middle class; but this is owing to the very simple reason that they have supplied the middle class with most of its new members; and what the middle class has thus gained in numbers the working class has lost. But, alike in point of aggregate income and average individual income, the progress of the middle class is altogether dwarfed by that of the working class—a progress the extent of which is absolutely unknown to the majority of our countrymen, but which forms probably the most extraordinary phenomenon in the social history of the world. The general outlines of this progress can be seen at a glance by referring to Fig. 8. The series of rising columns in both divisions of the figure represent the national income at the several dates named. The darker portions, at the bottom, represent the working class income; the lighter portions represent the incomes of the rich

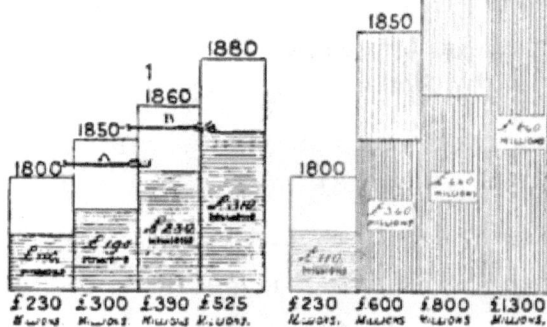

Fig. 8.

and the middle classes. Series 2 shows the actual growth of the whole actual income, which has risen from about £240,000,000 at the end of the last century to £1,300,000,000 (as was just stated) now; whilst the income of the working classes has risen from about £110,000,000 to £660,000,000. This actual increase, however, considered by itself, does not tell us the thing we are concerned to know; for the population having increased enormously as well as the wealth, we are left doubtful whether the poor have really secured larger individual incomes, or whether there are merely more of them with the same incomes or even smaller ones. The columns in Series 1 will make this point clear. Of the four columns comprised in it, the first represents the same thing as the first column in Series 2, namely, the income of the country in the year 1800. The other three columns in Series 1 represent, not the actual increase of the national income, but its increase *minus* the increase due to increased population: in other words, it represents the increased incomes produced by the same number of persons as constituted the whole population in 1800— that is to say, about 15,000,000. Here we get rid completely of all the confusion which the increase of population causes; and each step in the growth of the income, as represented thus, means a corresponding growth in the income of the individual. This figure exhibits two facts which, if one may judge by the language used by writers and public speakers whenever the Labour Question or the Social Question is discussed, are altogether unknown to the public of this country. The two facts are as follows:—During the first sixty years of this century the income of the working classes rose to such an extent that in the year 1860 it was equal (all deductions for the increase of population being made) to the income of all classes in the year 1800. This is indicated by the arrow A. But there is a far more extraordinary fact to follow, and that is, that a result precisely similar has been accomplished since in one-half of the time. In 1880 the income of the working classes was (all deductions for the increase of population being made) more than equal to the income of all classes in the year 1850. This is indicated by the arrow marked B. Thus, the working classes in 1860 were in precisely the same pecuniary position as the working classes in 1800 would have been had the entire wealth of the kingdom been in their hands; and the working classes of to-day are in a better pecuniary position than their fathers would have been could they have plundered and divided between them the wealth of every rich and middle-class man at the time of the building of the first great Exhibition. The wildest Socialist, the most discontented Radical, cannot possibly claim for the people more wealth than exists, no matter what revolution he might have it in his power to accomplish; and few Socialists imagine that it would be possible to redistribute everything. And yet, in actual fact, this miracle has taken place—has taken place twice in the course of three generations—and has taken place, not only without any attempt at revolution, but in consequence of those very institutions against which would-be revolutionists protest. The figure gives in round numbers the aggregate amount of the working-class income, and also the income of all classes, at the various dates indicated, both as they actually were for the whole population, and also as they were relative to a population of the same size.

In dealing with such vast sums as are at present in question, we must, of course, not look for any impracticable accuracy; but there is substantially a complete unanimity amongst statisticians with regard to the broad facts of the case, and the slight discrepancies between the respective calculations are so small that, if expressed in a diagram, the eye could hardly detect them.

These facts form a curious comment on a paper entitled "The Case for Labour," by a Labour member of the present House of Commons, which appeared in *The Pall Mall Magazine* a year or two ago. The whole of the writer's observations were coloured by that very fallacy to which I referred at starting—by the idea that, whatever might be the case with the rich and the middle classes, the working classes were constantly getting poorer, whilst the difficulties of finding occupation were becoming greater. The fallacy involved in this latter supposition is as great as that involved in the former; and those who are in doubt as to this point will do well to consult Professor Marshall's remarks on it in his *Principles of Economics*. It is unnecessary to dwell upon it here. It is sufficient to confine ourselves to the mere question of wages, and to insist once more on the fact that the vast body of the people—the working classes as distinguished from the rich and the middle classes—have increased in wealth more rapidly than any other class of the community, and that Mr. Giffen is perfectly right in saying that nearly the whole of the advantages gained during the past half-century have gone to them.

The sketch at the head of this chapter presents a sort of epitome of their history since the year 1800. The man represents the average labourer. The weight he is grasping represents the amount of work which the average labourer could do at the beginning of this century. The larger weights represent the constantly increasing amount of work which he has since become able to do, through the powers lent to him by the ability of others; and the flag standing by each of the weights indicates the average wages of such a labourer at the various periods mentioned. The condition of the wage-earners is illustrated yet further by Fig. 9, which embodies the results of Mr. Giffen's latest investigations. The column represents the proportions of the working classes in receipt of annual wages of the amounts stated.

It is idle for philanthropists, true or false—for those who sympathise with want and sorrow, or who affect sympathy—to attempt to disprove these facts by citing the cases of misery to be found in every town in the kingdom. London alone possesses an unfortunate class, which is probably as large as the whole population of Glasgow, and an endless procession of rags and tatters might be marched into Hyde Park to demonstrate every Sunday. But if the unfortunate class in London is as large as the whole population of Glasgow, we must not forget that the population of London is greater by nearly a million than the whole population of Scotland; and the great practical lesson which requires to be instilled into social reformers is that the tendencies of a civilisation must be studied in its effects for good on nine-tenths of the population, rather than in the absence of any such effects upon one-tenth; and that

FIG. 9.

£ 96.
£ 85.
£ 67.
£ 50.
£ 43.
£ 35.
£ 30. AND UNDER

the real problem to be solved is not how to alter these tendencies, but to bring those under their influence who have hitherto remained outside it. To attempt to interfere with the progress of the nine-tenths because the one-tenth has not hitherto shared it, would be like attempting to wreck a great steamer with six hundred passengers merely because sixty of them had bad accommodation in the steerage.

CHAPTER II

THE MINIMUM OF HUMANE LIVING

HAVING now seen the way in which wealth is tending to distribute itself, and how, in spite of all the phenomena of chronic poverty and periods of occasional distress, the working classes as a whole are constant gainers by the natural economic processes which are at work around us, and how the multiplication of large incomes is accompanied by a general rise in wages, let us pass on to consider the most recent doctrine of the modern labour party with regard to the means by which wages may be increased yet further—that is to say, the doctrine of the minimum wage, or, as it is now called, the " living wage."

In certain countries, and notably in Russia, the wages in factories are so low, and the hours of labour so long, that the commiseration of every Englishman, of whatever class, would be excited for the fate of operatives employed on such hard terms; and when we consider their case, and compare it with that of others in other countries, the conclusion becomes obvious to us that by some means or other—by the action of public opinion, or by raising the standard of living—it is possible so to increase the minimum rate of wages, and at the same time to decrease the maximum duration of the labour day, as to place the worst-paid operative in a better position than that at present occupied by his fellows generally in Russia.

We may therefore say that, within certain limits, and *with certain reservations*, the doctrine of the "living wage" embodies an important and practical truth. The only question at issue is, How, under any given circumstances, is the amount of the living wage to be determined? What is the annual sum, and what is the general condition as to food, clothing, house-accommodation, and so forth, below which it is reasonable and practicable to attempt to prevent the wages and general condition of the poorest classes of workmen from falling?

The urgent and definite character of this problem was brought home to this country in a very remarkable manner by the great coal-strike of a few years ago, in connection with which the doctrine of the living wage first came into prominence. The colliers, it will be remembered, struck against a certain reduction in their wages on various grounds, but on the following ground in particular—that it would not leave them enough to support them in what their leaders had taught them to call "a humane condition." It was not denied that it would leave them better off than their fathers had been, or than they themselves had been till a comparatively recent period. But according to their leaders this did not alter the question. A number of doctrinaires all over the country—some of them professional agitators, some of them emotional clergymen—began preaching the doctrine that "a humane condition" for a collier comprised all the comforts and superfluities which the colliers, as a class, had enjoyed during the period of their greatest prosperity; and this condition was put forward as the irreducible minimum of wellbeing, below which, if a collier sank, he was being defrauded of his rights as a man.

Now, was this way of putting the case a true

way or a false way? Was it in harmony with reason, and based on any principle capable of general application? Were the colliers who followed their leaders' teachings, and refused to accept the proposed reduction of wages, on the ground that it would deprive them of the means of leading "a humane life," acting as foolish and misguided men, recklessly unwilling to take the rough of life with the smooth? or were they fighting, as their leaders maintained they were, to prevent themselves and their families from sinking into a want and squalor that would be a disgrace to civilisation?

The real question that is here involved, though the great coal-strike brought it specially to the front, is involved equally in all our contemporary labour struggles, and in all our views and sentiments as to the condition of the great majority of the community, What is the standard by which we measure "a humane condition"? That is to say, what is the smallest income that will keep a human being and his family in such a condition that we can regard their existence with complaisance, that we can feel it to be a happiness to themselves and a benefit to the community, and any pity or complaint with regard to it to be entirely out of place?

About this question not only is the vaguest and most irrational language used by many people, but the vaguest ideas prevail, and the most irrational sentimentality is cherished. The persons who sin most in this way are generally persons belonging to the richer and more educated classes. These persons are accustomed to speak of the vast majority of mankind as deserving commiseration simply because they are obliged to lead that life of muscular labour which, under many conditions, is the necessary lot of all, and from which, under any conditions, only a minority can be exempt, and because they do not enjoy a number of luxuries and advantages which, from the very nature of the case, a minority only can possess. Some people, for instance, speak as if everybody was to be commiserated who did not possess servants. Now, a state is quite conceivable in which nobody possessed them; but it is obviously impossible, from the very nature of things, that in any state they should be possessed by more than a comparative few. What, then, can be more foolish and mischievous than to popularise standards of living which must, under any social arrangements possible, be necessarily out of the reach of the majority of those who aim at them? So, again, with regard to the question of labour: what is more common than the same commiserating tone applied to men because they have to dig, plough, fish, and be out in all weathers? How often are we invited to endeavour to alleviate their "hard lot"—to think of their "hard life"! Can any kind of sentiment be falser and more demoralising than this? It is based on the idea that the life of luxury is the rule, and the life of toil and exposure the exception. But everybody who thinks can see that the exact reverse is the case, and that toil and exposure not only are, but always have been, and always must be, the common, the typical human lot. And this was so before luxury ever existed, and it would be so still were all luxury abolished. It is idle to turn, as some people do, to the luxurious classes, and ask them what they would say if this life of toil were to be theirs? Many, no doubt, would whimper and bemoan themselves; others would bear the change with fortitude. But what the luxurious classes might do, or say, or think, in such an event has nothing to do with the matter. They would not alter the common lot by sharing it; and to say that daily toil is hard, and that exposure to weather is hard, is merely another way of saying that human life is hard. It may be hard if men choose to think it so; but by thinking it hard they only make it harder. *Durum, sed levius fit patientiâ.*

The lot, then, that is commonly called the lot of the poor is not, as such, a fit subject of any commiseration. It is the normal type of human life; and those foolish persons who treat it as if it were not so would do well to read what was said upon this subject by Cobbett—himself a son of the toiling classes—in his excellent little book, *Cottage Economy*. But these general considerations, in order to make them useful, require to be reduced to a more particular form. Though much that is called poverty deserves no commiseration, and though it is at once mischievous and cruel to attempt to make the mass of men discontented with it, yet poverty is a thing of many degrees; and there are degrees of it to which every Christian, every philanthropist, every statesman, will do his utmost to prevent any class falling. There is a certain minimum degree of wellbeing which it should be the main object of all statesmanship to secure; and it is impossible to insist on this fact too often, too publicly, or with too great and earnest emphasis. But the practical question is all a question of degree. What is this minimum standard of comfort and humane living, up to which we can hope to raise everybody, and below which we should endeavour to prevent any man's wages sinking? What does it depend upon?

One thing may be said at once—that it does not depend on what well-to-do philanthropists might think desirable; for it is limited at all events by one hard external circumstance, namely, the amount of income which would go to each family were the whole income, of whatever nation may be in question, divided equally amongst everybody. The minimum of humane living cannot possibly be more than that. But not only is the income of the same nation different at one period from what it is at another, but the incomes of different nations differ widely from each other at the same period. Thus the average income per head of the United Kingdom to-day is nearly three times that of Italy. Accordingly a philanthropist who was anxious to raise the minimum standard as high as possible all over Europe could not by any possibility raise it in Italy to much more than one-third of the height to which he could raise it in this country. The illustration on the opposite page will assist the reader in realising this important point. The houses of various sizes are in proportion to the respective amounts per head that could be yielded in each country by an equal division of its entire income. Suppose, then, we were to fix "the minimum standard of humane living" for a man in this country as the maximum that would come to everybody from an equal distribution of everything, we should be forced with regard to other European nations to conclude that it is impossible for them as nations to lead a humane existence at all; or else we must be prepared to say that a standard of living is quite fit for a *man* in Italy or Russia or Austria that would not be fit for a pig in England. We

UNITED KINGDOM.

FRANCE.

GERMANY.

AUSTRIA.

ITALY.

RUSSIA.

will, however, for the present waive this point, and confining our attention to our own country and the obvious limits placed on the standard of "humane living" by the limitation of the total income of the country, let us consider if it is not true that within these limits the standard of living depends on the habits and requirements which can be developed amongst the great masses of the people. Does it not depend on what certain clergymen, who affect the name of Christian Socialists, call "the divine discontent" of the people with their existing conditions? And may not the people in the long run be able to demand and get whatever, within the limits just specified, they can be taught to expect and want?

The answer to this question is as follows:— The standard of living does depend to a certain degree on the habits and requirements of the great masses of the people, and can to a certain degree be raised by educating their habits and amplifying their requirements. A population content with squalor and one-roomed cabins will no doubt demand and command less wages than a population to which the primary decencies of life are a necessity; and by educating men to be disgusted with indecency and filth, the minimum standard of humane living can be raised, and the wages of these men can be increased. But the progress that can be brought about in this way is progress that can be carried to a certain degree only; and this is a degree that not only falls far short of the limit fixed by the limits of the national income, but depends on, and is fixed by, a totally different order of facts. My object in this chapter is to explain in the clearest way possible what these facts are. It will be seen, when once we have grasped them, that they give us a "standard of humane living" which has nothing to do with personal sentiment or opinion, with the prejudices of Tories or the "aspirations" of Socialists, but is determined by forces and conditions which are the same for every school, and which no political reformer could even pretend that he will be able to modify.

The "minimum standard of humane living" is determined, and is necessarily determined, by the maximum *which a man who pays no rent can extract by his own labour from the worst soil under cultivation.* To persons unaccustomed to economic reasoning this statement may sound like academic jargon. I wish to show them that its meaning is of the simplest and of the homeliest kind, and that the most ordinary man or woman is as capable of giving an intelligent assent to it as the most unkempt and most untidy professor who ever held forth in a lecture-room.

Let us begin then with reminding ourselves of a few truisms. All life depends on food; nearly all our food comes from the soil; and therefore we could none of us live unless the soil were cultivated. In other words, no nation could exist if it were not for the existence of a class of cultivators somewhere. Men tilling the soil, therefore, must always be a social necessity; and it is impossible to conceive of any human society of which they do not form a prominent and essential part. Now let us, for simplicity's sake, accept the view of the Socialists that a capitalistic and employing class is a superfluity in agriculture; let us suppose that small owners, who employ nobody but themselves, and each of whom owns just as much land as he can himself cultivate, and no more, are capable of extracting the maximum produce from the soil, and that men of this class between them cultivate the entire country. Now let the reader consider what will be the situation of these men. It is obvious that they are men forming a necessary class, and enjoying the maximum degree of comfort that they could by any possibility attain, for they extract from the soil the utmost it can be made to yield; and everything which it yields is their own property, which they either actually consume themselves, or sell for their own benefit. Let us take, for instance, any one of these men and consider his case. The acres which he, or he and his family between them, own and cultivate yield, we will say, produce to the annual value of £100. Unless this man become a capitalistic employer of other men—a supposition which we are now expressly excluding—his income of £100 could not possibly be increased by so much as a single sixpence, except through the charity of the rest of the community. It could be raised to £105 only by the rest of the community giving him £5. In that case he would be yearly consuming so much more than he produced, and consequently his existence would be a disadvantage, a useless expense, a burden to all other classes. Now the existence of an individual of this kind might be tolerated; but the existence of a great productive class, thus dependent on other classes, not only could not be tolerated, but would be impossible. Every great productive class must be self-supporting. It must, to say the least, produce as much as it consumes, or, in other words, it must not consume more than it produces, or, in other words again, its standard of humane living must not exceed the value of its gross products. If the value of the gross products will not support the producers as human beings they ought to be set to produce something else. Thus, if the value of the gross agricultural products of this country would not be sufficient, supposing the whole of it were divided amongst the labourers, to support them in a state fit for human beings, the agriculture of this country ought to be extinguished, and we ought to get all our food from some other region; but if, on the other hand, we believe, what no sane person doubts, that the soil of this country ought to be cultivated, and ought not to become a desert, we must necessarily believe that the value of its gross products is, supposing that the labourers get the whole of it, at least sufficient to support them in a humane condition—a condition in which they are not objects of pity, and with which it would be folly and madness to attempt to make them discontented. Let us then put our minimum of humane living as high as we can, we cannot put it higher than the value of the entire products which agriculture yields the agriculturist who works his own soil, or a soil for which he pays no rent, with his own hands; and the value of these products will at once give us this highest minimum in pounds, shillings, and pence.

Now, however, we must consider another point. We have been speaking of the soil of this country, and a class of cultivators each owning just so much of it as he can cultivate. The reader knows, of course, even if he knows nothing of agriculture, that all soils are not equally good; but of the degree of difference between their qualities and the amount there is of land of each quality he probably has an exceedingly dim idea. Let him turn then to the accompanying diagram. It will give him a rough, but substantially accurate, idea of how the goodness of the soil in this country varies, and the proportion between the area of the best soils and the poorer. The entire oblong figure represents the whole cultivated area of the United Kingdom. The shaded portions represent the value of the soil as indicated by the rent paid for it, and the entire spaces between the various points marked A represent the

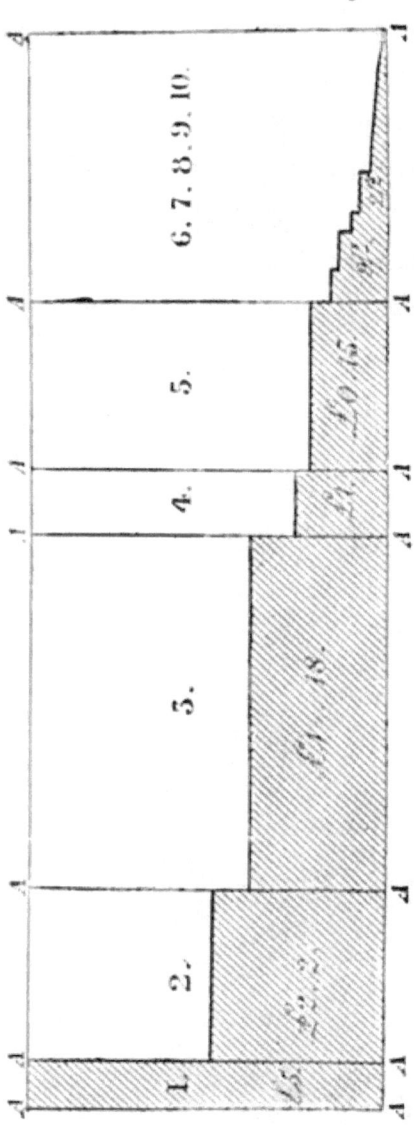

proportionate amounts of soils of each quality. Thus the best land—the land whose produce per acre fetches the largest price (such as dairy land and market-garden land near towns), and the rental of which, sometimes as high as £12,

A   B

averages £5 : 12s.—forms hardly so much as one twenty-sixth of the country. Land of quality 2 forms not so much as one-sixth, whilst land of quality 4 and of qualities yet inferior, forms, roughly speaking, one-half of the cultivated surface of Great Britain and Ireland.

Now, what is the meaning of this fact as related to our present inquiry? Its meaning is this: that if the agriculturists of this country were a body each member of which owned as much soil as he himself could cultivate, and, appropriating in this way the full value of the products, were to enjoy (as we have seen he would do) the maximum income possible for a self-supporting cultivator, the incomes of one-half of the agriculturists of this kingdom would be less than half the incomes of the other half, and the incomes of one-tenth would be less than a fifth of the incomes of another tenth. A parent, for instance, has a son called Tommy, destined to be an agriculturist and capable of cultivating twelve acres.[1] Tommy's income will depend on the quality of the twelve acres allotted to him. Let us represent his income by the proportions of his figure, and we shall see that if he has twelve acres of quality 1 he will be the rotund personage marked A, in the drawing on the preceding page, whereas if his acres are of one of those poorer qualities which together make

---

[1] Where certain inferior soils are in question, the area would have to be more than twelve acres, for the unit is really determined by the area which one man can cultivate to the best advantage; but there are many soils of widely different productivity, which would require per acre the same amount of labour.

LAND OF QUALITY 1.

LAND OF QUALITY 2.

LAND OF QUALITY 3.

LAND OF QUALITIES 4 AND 5.   LAND OF QUALITIES 6, 7, 8, 9, AND 10.

up an entire half of the United Kingdom, he will not bulk larger in our sight than the portrait of him marked B.

And now let us employ this same method of illustration further. Let us suppose, as before, the whole of our agricultural population to consist of cultivators each owning as much soil as he can cultivate; and let us represent them, according to their incomes, as Tommies of various sizes. The result will be substantially that which is shown in the series of pictures on p. 53. For every two Tommies such as those who cultivate and grow fat on land of quality 1, we shall have nine less fat cultivating land of quality 2; we shall have eighteen less fat still on land of quality 3, and twenty-four of varying degrees of meagreness on land of qualities 4, 5, 6, 7, 8, 9, and 10.

The reader will now see the meaning of the statement that the minimum standard of humane living cannot by any possibility be made to exceed the value of the produce which a man who pays no rent can exact by *his own labour from the worst soil under cultivation.* This principle does not in the least conflict with the doctrine that the condition of the labouring class can be improved by raising their standard of living. We must, on the contrary, take it in connection with this doctrine, and see the consequences that follow. Let us turn, then, to the figures in our picture who represent the cultivators of the worst land cultivated—land of qualities 6, 7, 8, 9, and 10, the rental of which varies from nine shillings to a shilling an acre; and let us suppose we decide that their incomes are too small for their comfort, their health, their happiness—in a word, for "humane living." How can these men's standard of living be raised? They already take and consume every penny they produce by their utmost skill and exertion. How are we to add to their incomes? We can do this in one way only: by taking them off the poor soil they occupy and finding for them some more lucrative occupation. But in doing this what should we be doing? We could not transfer them to any more productive soils, because, *ex hypothesi*, all the more productive soils are already occupied. We should, therefore, whatever other occupation we found for them, be declaring in the most emphatic way imaginable that such and such a proportion of the cultivated soil of this kingdom ought to be cultivated no longer by anybody, but allowed forthwith to relapse into a state of wilderness; for we should be declaring that it could not by any possible means support its cultivators in a condition fit for human beings. We may therefore, if we like, raise our standard of humane living as far as the limits of the national income will permit; but we must remember that the moment it exceeds the standard supplied by the gross incomes derived from the worst soil cultivated we are condemning such soil to go out of cultivation altogether.

Let us see how this would work out. The average yearly value of the total agricultural products of this kingdom is about £220,000,000; the total cultivated area is about 70,000,000 acres; thus the total produce per acre averages about £3. The average rental for the whole kingdom is under £1 an acre. We are therefore safe in saying that a man who cultivates the kind of land that lets now for £1 an acre will not produce per acre more than £3. Let us assume—this is merely an assumption—that he can cultivate sixteen acres. In that case his income will be £48. And now let us suppose that some friend to labour endeavours to benefit his kind by raising the standard of living, and persuading the labouring classes that a life fit for a self-respecting man cannot be supported on £48 a year. This will mean that at least one-half of the soil of the United Kingdom ought to go out of cultivation. The whole of the figures in the bottom row of our picture ought to be swept at once out of the ranks of agriculturists. We need only raise our standard a little higher, and we shall have to sweep away likewise the row of figures given above them. Then we should have to cease, because the incomes of the men cultivating soils of the first and second qualities would be more than the sums that could come to them from an equal division of the entire income of the nation; but if we were only to raise our standard thus far, we should, as the reader will see by referring to the oblong diagram on p. 50, be declaring that three-quarters of the national soil was incapable of supporting its cultivators, and ought to be allowed to return to a state of nature.

Will anybody be silly enough to make such

a proposition as that? We may safely say that nobody will; or if any one did, certainly no one would listen to him. Will anybody say that so much as half the soil of the kingdom should be allowed to go out of cultivation? There is just as little chance of anybody's saying that. Indeed, when we consider that some of the bitterest attacks on the existing landed class have been made in consequence of the removal of agricultural populations from land in Scotland and elsewhere the rent of which was under five shillings an acre, we may say that practically there is no one, of whatever party, who maintains that any considerable portion of even the poorest land in this country should be allowed to go out of cultivation. There is therefore an implied agreement between all parties, whether all parties are aware of the fact or no, that the poorest of our cultivated soils, if only they were rent-free, would yield to each of their cultivators produce of sufficient value to support him in a "humane condition," a condition, moreover, which could not be improved unless he abandoned the soil in question, and with which therefore he ought to be contented.

It is not proposed here to suggest any precise figure as that of the minimum income which ought to content the cultivator. It may be observed, however, that much of the poorest land of this country bears so low a rental as to be very nearly rentless already, and is already cultivated by peasant holders. Thus, if we were to turn these men into owners and let them keep their rent themselves, their incomes would be somewhat, but not greatly, increased. If therefore we wish to keep these men in their holdings, to attach them to the soil, and to perpetuate them as a class, we are, consciously or unconsciously, affirming that the incomes which they enjoy at present are sufficient, or are within a fraction of being sufficient, to support a life not only fit for a human being, but a life which we can feel satisfaction in thinking that human beings lead. We thus arrive at a definite objective standard, entirely independent of sentimental opinion or class feeling, by which to fix the minimum of humane living.

In all industrial disputes, then, when any question arises as to the attitude of labourers in resisting a reduction of wages, the public and the men themselves, and especially their leaders who have theories, will do well to refer to the standard of a sufficient income supplied by the utmost income that can be earned by this class of cultivators—an income which half the agitators in the country have been virtually declaring to be sufficient by denouncing those who would drive these men off the soil. That a large portion of the labouring class may raise itself to indefinitely greater opulence is not denied for a moment. It has indeed already done so, as was shown in the first chapter of this volume; and there is hope that in the future it may raise itself still farther. There is hope also that even the cultivators of the poorest soils may, with improvements in industrial methods, earn larger incomes. It must further be borne in mind that the cost of living varies in different localities, and also the kind and quality of food required by men in different occupations: therefore the living wage of a Highland crofter, for instance, would not be a living wage for an operative in a manufacturing town. But these considerations do not affect the general principle that has been just explained, namely, that the minimum standard of decent, or "humane" living, in any given country, and any given state of civilisation, cannot be generally far removed from the standard supplied by the living of that part of the population, who, in accordance with their own wishes, and with the sanction of the rest of the community, occupy the poorest soils under cultivation, and paying either no rent, or merely a nominal rent for them, consume the whole, or virtually the whole of the product.

We will now proceed to consider a yet wider question than the above, namely, a set of conditions inherent in every society, socialistic or individualistic, wherein division of labour prevails, by which all wages, whether sufficient or insufficient, are limited.

CHAPTER III

WAGES AND THE PRODUCTS OF WORK

Mr. Bright once said that the secret of convincing oratory was to say one thing, and say it over and over again. Let us so far be guided by him as to say over again, in general terms, the gist of what has been said already with regard to the living wage; for we shall find that that subject connects itself very closely with the wider one on which we shall presently be entering.

We have just seen that if we took the same labourer, and settled him, during successive years, on soils of different quality, that his income, *cæteris paribus*, would each year be different. Let us then fix our attention on the smallest of these incomes, namely, that which he would derive from the poorest of the soils allotted him. We will suppose this to be such soil as in certain parts of the country is now let at something like a shilling an acre. The man's rent, whatever it comes to, is really part of the produce of the soil rented. We will accordingly represent the total produce by the oblong figure A. In the case of soils like these, which are just on the margin of cultivation, a very small proportion of the produce is paid away in rent, the larger part being necessary for the bare support of the cultivator. The man's rent, therefore, will be indicated with substantial accuracy by the small shaded portion at the top of Fig. 1. Now, it is evident that if this man is to earn his own living on the soil in question, his total income cannot possibly be increased—the general condition of the industrial arts remaining the same—except by remitting his rent to him, or giving him the soil for his own; and, in this case, his income will be increased by the amount indicated by the shaded portion of the figure, but it cannot by any possibility be increased farther. If, then, the public is contented that such soil should be cultivated at all, the public virtually affirms that the cul-

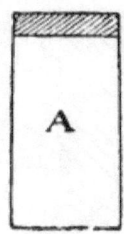
Fig. 1.

tivator should be contented with such a life as can be supported by the consumption or sale of the total produce which it yields to him.

To render this point and its significance yet more clear, let us take our parallelogram A, in Fig. 1, which represents the cultivator's income on the poorest soil, and place it, as in Fig. 2, beside corresponding

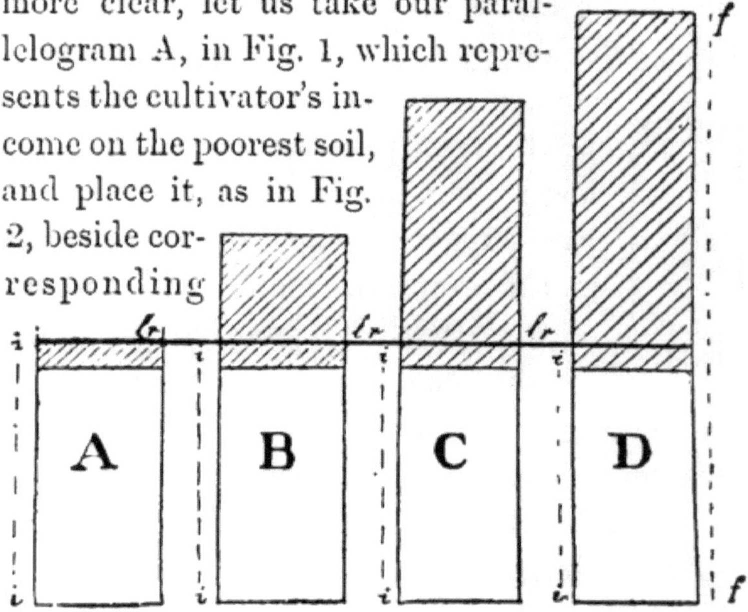

FIG. 2.

parallelograms, which will represent his income on superior soils. The entire parallelogram A, we must remember, including the shaded portion, represents at once the total produce of the soil in question, and also an income on which a man can support a life with which, in the judgment of his contemporaries, he ought to be contented. If the parallelogram A, then, represents the total which the man can produce from the poorest soil, the total which by similar labour he can extract from superior soil will be represented by the parallelograms B, C, and D. Now let us suppose that at starting the cultivator of the poorest soil pays away in rent the portion of his produce represented by the shaded portion of the parallelogram A, and that then some measure of land-reform frees him from this payment, and makes his holding practically his own, on the ground that thus he is able to lead a humane life, and that otherwise he would not be able. The sole result of such legislation on other and better land would not be to free it of rent likewise, but only to reduce the rent of it by the precise amount paid for the poorest holding. For instance, to free land, which is now rented at two shillings an acre, of all rent, would be merely to reduce land that now lets at five guineas an acre to a rental of five pounds three shillings. How this is can be seen easily from the diagram. The dotted line $i\ i$ represents a minimum living income. Let the dark horizontal line $l\ r$ represent the measure of land-reform by which the cultivator of the poorest soil is allowed to retain the whole of his rent. The same line, when it crosses the other figures, merely cuts off a small fraction of the portions which represent their original rents; and it cannot possibly do more. If the cultivator of the poorest soil will obtain a living income by adding to his original income the shaded portion of A, it cannot be maintained that the cultivators of the superior soils will not be able to support a humane existence unless we make over to them the whole of the shaded portion of B, C, and D. We can soon see this by taking the cultivator of the best soil, and trying to apply to his case the reasoning that was applied to that of the cultivator of the worst. The total value of his products is represented by the parallelogram D. If we say of him that he cannot support a humane existence unless he has the whole of the shaded portion added to his original income, we shall be saying that a living income, or the minimum wage, is represented not by the line ii, but by the line ff. In that case it would follow that the inferior soils could not be cultivated at all, because their total produce would, as has been said already, be insufficient to yield a living income to their cultivators. But since we assume that in the judgment of the entire nation the inferior soils still ought to be cultivated, the living income must necessarily be limited by the total product which results from a man's labour when applied not to the best soil cultivated, but to the worst.

Let us, then, continue to fix our attention on this minimum living income of the cultivator of the poorest soil, and ask ourselves the following question with regard to it: Is it a minimum which there is no hope of increasing? And does the cultivator of the poorest soil stand accordingly outside the ranks of progress? If we take the working men of this country as a whole, the increase of their average incomes has, during the past hundred years, been constant and almost incredible. Has the cultivator of the poorest soil had no share in this increase? Is his position no better than it was a hundred years ago? And is there no hope that fifty years hence it may be better than it is now? The answer to these questions is that his position during the past hundred years has become better, and may continue to grow better still; and in two ways. The first way is obvious, namely, by the discovery of improved methods of agriculture, which will enable him with the same labour to extract more produce from the soil. The second way is altogether different. It is by an increase, not in the amount of his products, but in their selling price or their exchangeable value. Of the first way I do not propose to speak. I am going to deal solely with the

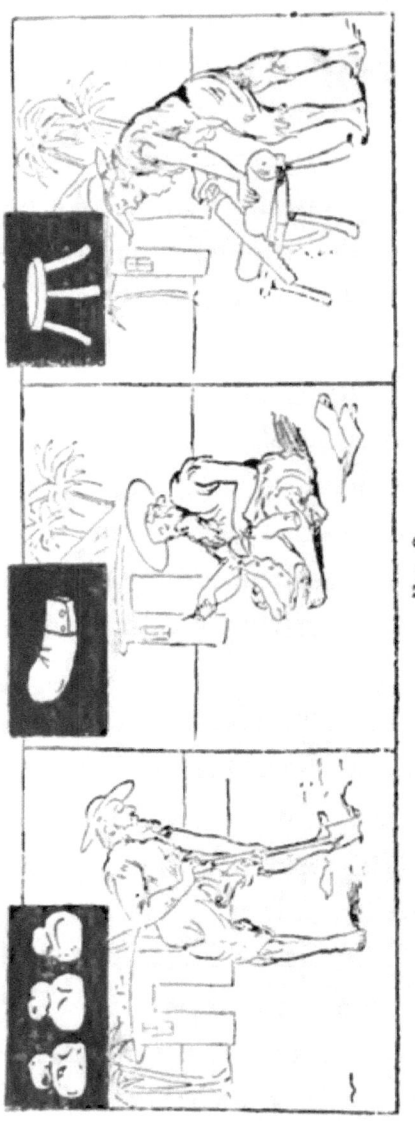

Fig. 3.

second; and if I can make the reader clearly understand that, I shall have made him understand the real truth of the question which is at the bottom of nearly all the labour disputes which are now impeding industry.

As every one knows, the most rudimentary form of progress has been some simple division of labour. Instead of each man producing everything that he himself needs, different sets of men devote themselves to producing severally some one kind of commodity which they all need. Instead of each man producing his own bread, his own coats, and his own furniture, one man tills the soil and produces bread for three, another sews and produces clothes for three, another works as a carpenter and produces stools and tables for three. Now, if each man produced all that he wanted for himself, the measure of his income would be the amount of the things produced by him; but the moment this arrangement ceases, and its place is taken by a division of labour, his position in this respect altogether changes, and the measure of his income is not the amount or even the quality of the things produced by him, but the amount and quality of the other things which he can get in exchange for them. It is no doubt true that where industry is in a very rude stage and only necessaries are produced, each man will keep and consume part of his own produce. But this is not an essential feature in the case. Even in a very rude community we can easily imagine a man who never smoked getting his living by the manufacture of tobacco. We will, however, in order to make our argument clearer, not give this fact a place in it.

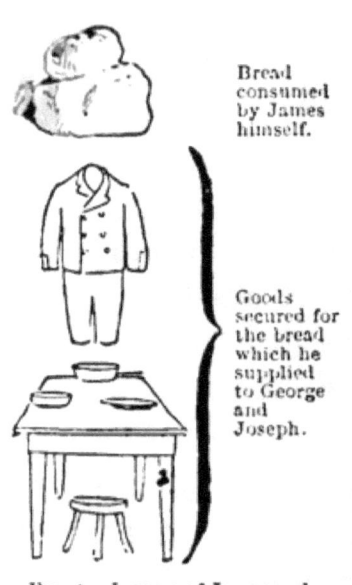

Fig. 4.—Income of James under Condition No. 1.

(Bread consumed by James himself. Goods secured for the bread which he supplied to George and Joseph.)

Let us then imagine a community of three men, each living in a house, which we will assume to be provided for him, and wanting nothing but food, clothes, and furniture. One man cultivates the soil, raises corn, and makes bread; another makes clothes out of the skins of wild animals which he catches; a third fells timber, and makes chairs, tables, and other utensils. We will call these men James, George, and Joseph; and Fig. 3, p. 68, which represents each of them, with the results of a day's labour in the corner—in one case three loaves, in another the sleeve of a shirt, and in another a three-legged stool—will help to impress them on the imagination of the reader. We will begin with considering the position of James, the cultivator and bread-producer. He produces, we will say, by the utmost expenditure of his labour, three loaves a day, every loaf representing a man's daily consumption. It is impossible for him, by any method of agriculture with which he is acquainted, to obtain more loaves from any soil accessible to him; therefore, so far as the quantity of his produce is concerned, he has no hope of increasing it, nor in respect of the loaves which he consumes himself is there any possibility of his position being changed at all. These loaves, however, form but one-third of his income. The remainder consists of loaves for which he has no use himself, but which happen to be necessary to the existence of George and Joseph; he therefore gives a loaf daily to each of these men, and they return him an equivalent in clothes and household goods. James's income, therefore—or the amount of goods which he can secure for himself by his own labour—depends principally not on what his own products are, but on what the products of George and Joseph are, and on how much of these they will each give him in return for a daily loaf. Now, when men like these are working for the barest necessaries and the rudest comforts of existence, and all presumably work equally hard and well, their products will exchange in proportion to the time employed in producing them. Thus each loaf produced daily by James represents a third of his working day; therefore the clothes which, with one loaf

Bread consumed by James himself.

Goods secured for the bread supplied to George and Joseph.

FIG. 5.—Income of James under Condition No. 2.

daily—or 365 loaves during the year—he will be able to purchase from George, will be as many as George can make during one-third of the year, or four months; and the amount of furniture he can purchase from Joseph will be determined in the same way. Let us suppose, then, that in the third part of a year George can produce one complete outfit of clothes, and Joseph can produce a table, a three-legged stool, and a set of wooden dishes. James's income for such a year will be the 365 loaves he consumes himself, one outfit of clothes, a table, a three-legged stool, and a set of wooden dishes. This condition of things is illustrated in Fig. 4, p. 70.

But now let us suppose that whilst James's own labour and its immediate products undergo no change whatever—whilst James still works as he has done hitherto, and produces the same loaves daily, clothes-making and carpentry, by some miracle, both of them become easier; so that George, in the third part of a year, produces not only one outfit of clothes, but a pillow, a bolster, and a stuffed quilt also, and Joseph in the same time produces an arm-chair and two spoons, besides the table, the stool, and the wooden dishes. In this case James, in return for the loaves with which he supplies George and Joseph, will receive, in addition to what he received before, a pillow, a bolster, a stuffed quilt, two spoons, and an arm-chair, as is shown in the picture of his income "under condition No 2," Fig. 5, p. 72.

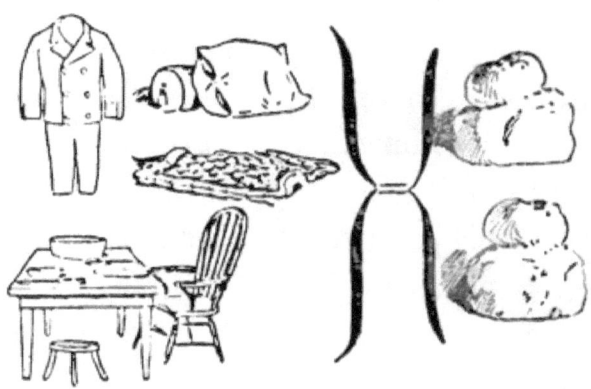

Fig. 6.

It is true that in actual life such changes as these are not brought about by miracles; but the preceding simple illustration will make it quite clear to the reader how an art such as agriculture may remain comparatively stationary whilst all other arts progress; and yet the agriculturist's income, without any effort of his own, may be augmented by an increase due to the progress of other arts. There is a good deal implied in all this which we will consider presently; but first, as an aid in doing so, let us realise the following point.

The increase we have just been supposing in the income of our imaginary peasant cultivator is merely the increase with which

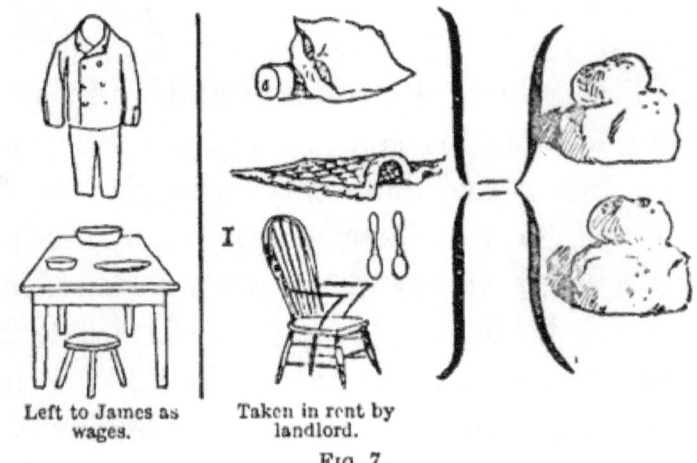

Left to James as wages.   Taken in rent by landlord.

FIG. 7.

we are all familiar under the name (so misleading because it has been so arbitrarily restricted to land) of the "unearned increment." Were the bread-producing industries of this country protected from all foreign competition, the whole country would ring at once with the accounts given by Radicals of the monstrous additional income that would be poured into the landlords' pockets. But this increment, the genesis of which would be so obvious in the case of the landlords, would take place just the same if *all landlordism were abolished*, and if the whole soil of the country were tilled by peasants owning it. The income of the agricultural landlord is simply a part of the value of the gross agricultural products, or, as we call them for simplicity's sake, of a certain number of loaves produced from his land, no matter how; and to the rest of the community, who give goods in exchange for these loaves, it makes no matter whatever how these goods are divided: whether, as in Fig. 6, p. 74, the whole of them go to James the cultivator, and his income is raised, as we supposed it to be, from its original small amount; or whether, as in Fig. 7, p. 75, the whole of this supposed increase —that is to say, the articles marked I—is taken by a landlord, and James is left in his original position. And, with regard to every kind of commodity, from the point of view of the entire community, except that particular fraction of it by which the commodity in question is manufactured, the same thing is true. Let us, for instance, take the case of clothing and bedding. To get a certain amount of these, James, as we have just seen, has to give George a specified number of loaves. It makes no matter to James what George does with them, whether he eats them all himself or shares them with a boy who helps him.

Here, then, comes the point which I wish to impress on the reader. It makes no matter whatever to our present argument whether James, George, and Joseph are taken to represent a composite body of capitalists and wage-earners, and their incomes to represent a total of wages and profits; or whether we eliminate the capitalist from our conception altogether, and assume each workman to be his own employer, and to receive as wages the entire amount of goods which comes to him in exchange for those which he himself produces. Our illustration, therefore, will, for our present purpose, be just as true to the facts of the present day if we assume the gross income of every industry to consist altogether of wages taken by the workmen.

We are now able to translate what has been

said about James's income into the current language of the day. That income—or, as we will now call it, his wages—consisted, as we saw, of the one loaf he ate himself and the goods which he received in exchange for two loaves. Thus two-thirds of his wages consisted, not of a constant quantity of goods he produced himself, but of the varying quantity of other goods which he got in exchange for them. The amount of the goods he got in exchange was neither more nor less than the price at which his goods sold. The reader will at last see, if he has not seen it before, what is the precise point at which I am aiming, namely, the relationship between wages and prices; and it will be apparent, from the illustrations given, that in any community in which there is division of labour, wages are not only related to prices, but they actually are prices. They are either the whole or some proportion of the assorted aggregate of commodities received in return for some one commodity by the producer of it.

Such being the case, the question which I shall ask the reader to consider is this: Are prices regulated by what the producer considers that his wages ought to be? or are his wages regulated by what the purchaser considers that prices ought to be? It is impossible to illustrate this question better than by referring once again to the last great coal-strike, which has already been mentioned as a great object lesson in economics. What the leaders in that strike endeavoured to teach the colliers was, that the prices of coal could be regulated by the colliers' habits and requirements to such an extent that their wages should never fall below a sum which had been fixed arbitrarily, which, compared with the wages of other industries, was exceptionally high, and which had not been obtained by the men till within comparatively recent years. This question is involved in nearly all the industrial struggles of the day; and it is specially desirable that all who would deal with such struggles, or form an opinion about the rights and wrongs of them, should master the rudiments of it thoroughly. It was not peculiar to the coal-strike. The coal-strike is taken solely as a striking and convenient illustration.

The real bearings of this question are

constantly obscured by the introduction of the question of the masters' profits; and the first great truth which should always be put before the public on the occasion of any struggle to make wages regulate prices is, that the masters' profits, or the fact of there being any masters in the case at all, has nothing to do with the point fundamentally at issue. A strike such as that of the colliers is really a strike, not against the masters, but the public. The masters are merely the intermediaries through whom the blow is transmitted. This has been already explained by the aid of Figs. 6 and 7; but it is so essential for the reader to understand the matter thoroughly, that I will explain it again, with the aid of a fresh set of illustrations. In the adjoining figure (8) we have two parallelograms of equal size, one of which represents a given quantity of coal, and the other, P P, the total price (whether we think of this as money or goods)

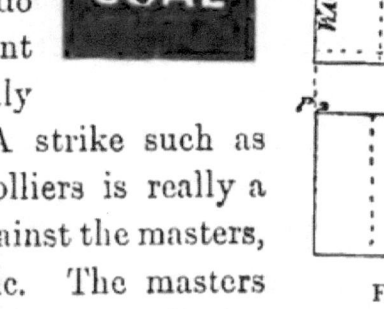

Fig. 8.

for which it exchanged in the year 1890; and we have a similar parallelogram, $P_2 P_2$, which represents the reduced price of the same quantity of coal at the end of the year 1893. Now, the sums represented by either of these parallelograms must all go in wages, or else be divided, as in P P, into wages and profits by some such line as a, b, or c; and profits must, in the opinion of the Trade Union leaders, be a legitimate portion of the total receipts, or not. If not, then the whole ought to go in wages, and when the workmen have got their rights, prices and wages will be co-extensive, so that any fall or rise in prices will be merely another expression for a fall or rise in wages. But if, on the other hand, profits *are* legitimate, and necessarily form some fraction, no matter how small, of the total receipts, the relation of wages to prices will remain just the same. A fall in prices, for instance, from 24 to 18 would diminish wages in exactly the same proportion, whether the whole of each sum went in wages or only five-sixths of it. Wages would fall from 24 to 18 in the one case, and from 20 to 15 in the other, and would depend on prices in either case just the same. We shall therefore be simplifying the question, without in any degree altering it, if we treat the total amount of coal produced by any given number of colliers in a given time as being entirely their own property, and consider their wages as the total of the commodities which they will get from the rest of the public in exchange for that coal. Now, in 1890 the public were willing to give commodities to an amount represented by the parallelogram P P for an amount of coal represented by the black parallelogram that corresponds to it; and in 1893 they were willing to give only commodities to the amount represented by the parallelogram $P_2 P_2$, which last is less than the former by an amount represented by the parallelogram, with dotted outlines, D. The whole problem, then, is a problem which has to do with the amount of commodities represented by the parallelogram D. As a matter of fact, the public refused any longer to part with these, and yet demanded from the colliers the same amount of coals; and the colliers' question is this : Can they by combination among themselves compel the public in exchange for this same amount of coals to give them daily this amount of commodities, which, for some reason or other, the public wished to withhold? The Trade Union leaders have been teaching the colliers that they can. They have been teaching them, in other words, that prices can be regulated by wages, instead of wages being obliged to follow prices. How far is such teaching true? This is the point that I am anxious to make clear.

I ask "*How far* is it true?" instead of asking whether it is true or false, because within certain limits it is true beyond all doubt, and is only false when these limits are passed. Let us first consider a set of circumstances under which it would be entirely true. We can do this more conveniently by referring again to Fig. 3, and again presenting to our imagination a community of three persons, James, George, and Joseph, each of whom produces enough for three persons of one of the prime necessaries of life, each keeping a third of what he himself produces and taking a third of the products of the other two. Now, what each of these men takes of the products of the other two has a double aspect. It is at once prices and wages. It is prices as seen by the man who parts with it; it is wages as seen by the man who takes it. Thus, when James, as shown in Fig. 4, gives one-third of his breadstuffs to George and receives a coat in return for them, the coat is the price which is paid for the bread by George, and it is the wages which James receives for his labour in producing the bread. Now, the prices in a community like this must follow wages—that is to say, their amount must conform to the wants of the recipient of the exchanged commodities. The goods of which they consist must, to use the phrase of the moment, be of such an amount as to constitute "a living wage"; and the reason is obvious. In such a community as this each man of the three imperatively requires a third of what each of the other two can give him, in order to live at all, or, at all events, to live in a condition which will enable him to produce goods which are similarly necessary for the others.

And now, bearing this in mind, let us amplify our community as follows. Let us impute to its members one new want, namely, coal. Let us imagine their climate such that, without a fire in his cottage, neither James nor George nor Joseph would be able to preserve his life; and let us accordingly add to them a fourth companion, Thomas, who is just able, by working as hard as the others, to provide himself and them with just as much coal as is necessary, but only just as much. In order to make the presence of Thomas possible, we must assume that James is able to make four loaves instead of three, that George is able to make four suits of clothes instead of three, and that Joseph similarly can make additional furniture. What, then, will be the position of Thomas? Besides the coal which he keeps for his own fire, he will require, in order to keep himself alive, a fourth of the furniture produced by Joseph, a fourth of the clothes produced by George, and a fourth of the bread produced by James. He will, that is to say, require to receive these things as the wages of his labour, and the others will, accordingly, be obliged to give them to him as the price of his coals. Thus, in a simple community of the kind we have imagined, prices not only can but must be kept at a point that will yield a certain wage to the producer.

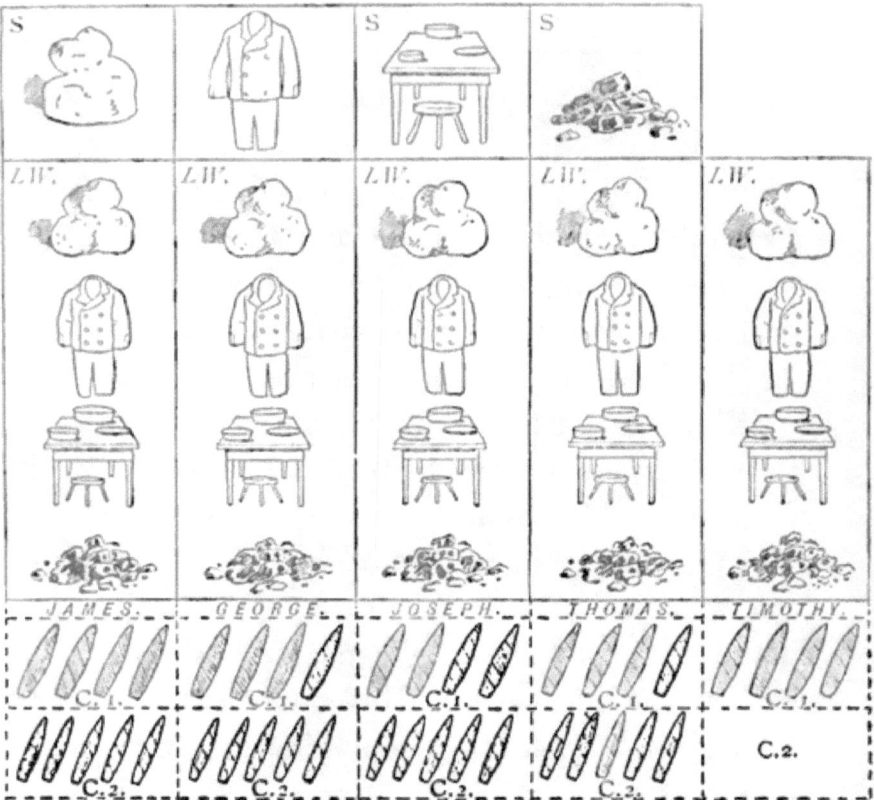

Fig. 9. Fig. 9a.

S S S S, Surplus articles, which may either be consumed as luxuries by the producers, or given to Timothy in exchange for cigars, as in Fig. 9 A.

L W, "The living wage" of the producer, as described in the text.

C 1, Cigars produced by Timothy, distributed in one possible way.

C 2,   „   „   „   distributed in another possible way.

But the reason of this fact is almost as obvious as its necessity. The reason is, that in the case with which we are dealing the requisites of life are the same for everybody concerned, and each requisite is for each man equally and absolutely necessary. But the moment such a community begins to make any advance, and, by learning more of the arts of cultivation and manufacture, becomes able to provide itself with any articles of comfort and luxury—with anything beyond the inevitable necessaries we have been considering—the relation of prices and wages begins to undergo a change. I will explain this by a very simple illustration. Let us suppose our community to have advanced so far in the arts that each of its four members, without any additional effort, can now produce five articles for every four that he produced formerly. Thus James has daily an extra loaf of bread and Thomas has daily fuel for an extra fire (see S S S S, Fig. 9). Now these extra articles are capable of being regarded and treated in one or the other of two totally different ways. They may be regarded and used as luxuries by the four men producing them—James, for instance, overeating himself on two loaves, and Thomas toasting himself at a fire that is twice as big as formerly; or they may be regarded and used as a complete set of necessaries, capable of sustaining the life of some fifth producer. Now let us suppose that at this juncture a fifth producer—Timothy—appears on the scene, who is capable of producing tobacco to the amount, let us say, of twenty cigars daily, and offers to supply the others with them in return for a supply of necessaries like those on which the others sustain themselves. Let the reader observe how now we have an entirely new situation. Timothy's position with regard to James, George, Joseph, and Thomas is fundamentally different to what theirs is with regard to one another. These four must all combine to keep each other alive, and must therefore pay prices which will yield each other a certain wage; but Timothy and his cigars are not necessary, and there is no reason, so far as they are concerned, why they should do anything to keep him alive at all. Let us suppose that none of them liked smoking, or that Timothy's cigars were very rank, and made them sick. Why should Thomas, for instance, deprive himself of the luxury of a fire all night, in order to purchase something which he would far rather be without? It is evident, then, that the first question with regard to Timothy is, not what wage shall he get, but whether he shall get any wage at all. Let us suppose, however, that Thomas and his three coadjutors try Timothy's cigars and like them. Thomas thinks on the whole that he gets more pleasure from smoking than he does from an extra fire; George would sooner have a cigar in his mouth daily than a new suit of clothes twice instead of once a year; and James and Joseph come to conclusions of a like kind. Each, therefore, decides to offer Timothy the extra fifth part of his own particular products, and thus between them to supply him with a living wage. The situation is shown clearly in Fig. 9. The four contiguous columns L W represent the living wage, or the actual necessaries of life, for the four original producers. The articles above these, S S S S, represent their surplus products, which they may either consume as luxuries or offer to

Timothy, as shown in the detached column (Fig. 9A), as the price of his cigars. That minimum price they must give him; but now comes the vexed question. Each of the other producers keeps one-fifth of the goods produced by him for his own use. Shall Timothy be allowed to keep one-fifth of his cigars for his own smoking (as shown in the arrangement C 1), in which case the five men will have four cigars each, and the wages of all be equal? or will he be obliged to give away the whole of them (as shown in the arrangement C 2), in which case each of the other men would have five cigars, and Timothy himself none, and thus the other men's wage would be 25 per cent more than his? The answer to this question rests altogether with the consumers. If they decide to have cigars at all, they must pay Timothy a price for them which will enable him to keep body and soul together; but whether they allow him to keep so much as a single cigar for himself depends altogether, not upon him, but them. It depends on the degree of pleasure which these men find in smoking. The more the reader considers this, the more clearly will he see the truth of it.

Let us, for instance, take the case of the collier Thomas. He, every day, has a day's surplus fuel—let us call it 50lb. This is the minimum price he can pay so as to get any cigars at all, for without it the cigar-maker could not be kept alive. The point at issue is, How many cigars will he demand for it? Four, or five? In one case the price of each cigar will be 8lb. of coal, in the other 10lb.; and as it is entirely a matter of choice with him whether he buys any, he is the arbiter of what price he will pay.

And now let us view the matter from Timothy's standpoint, not Thomas's. Let us suppose that Timothy finds some other means of warming himself, and thus the collier's coal becomes a luxury to the cigar-maker, just as the cigar-maker's cigars are a luxury to the collier. The cigar-maker now can turn tables on the collier; and just as the collier in the first case could fix the price of cigars, so in the second the cigar-maker can fix the price of coals. The price will depend on the difference between the pleasure which he feels he will derive from the warmth of a coal fire, and the pleasure which he feels he will derive from warmth obtained by some other means; and, having settled with himself what this difference is, he will weigh it with the pleasure which he will derive from smoking his own cigars.

Here at last we have a virtually exact counterpart to the actual position of the colliers in this country as related to the price-paying public. For the public a certain amount of coal is indeed a necessity, either directly, for domestic consumption, or indirectly, for the production of necessaries; but by far the larger part that is actually consumed is consumed for the sake of producing comforts and conveniences, either directly, on the consumer's hearth, or indirectly, in the production of commodities; and domestic consumption, though a small part of the total consumption, is yet a complete type of it. In Fig. 8 coal was represented by a black parallelogram. Let us now represent it by a parallelogram again, but let us subdivide this, and analyse it, as in Fig. 10, into a kitchen fire, which represents a necessary, a sitting-room fire, which represents comfort, and a library fire, which represents luxury; and let us say that these fires consume $\frac{1}{2}$ cwt. each, or $1\frac{1}{2}$ cwt. in the aggregate. And now let us place this parallelogram, as in Fig. 11, just above another, P P, which shall represent the price paid for thus much coal in the year 1890; and we will suppose this price, if expressed in goods, to be two chops, two

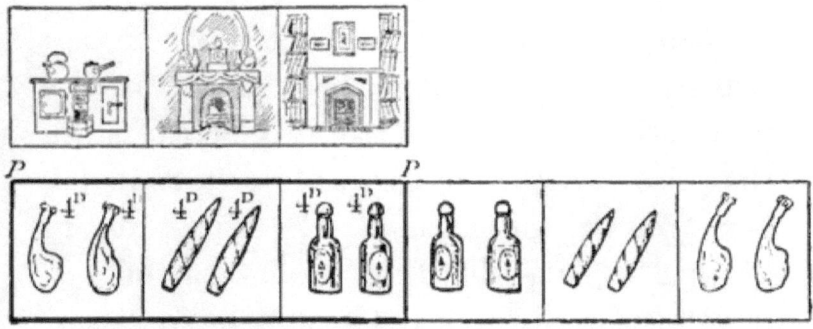

FIG. 10.

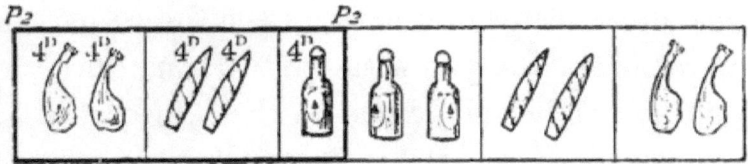

FIG. 11.

cigars, and two bottles of beer. The consumer is willing to pay this for three fires, because the total income which he is able to spend is sufficient to leave him, when he has done so, a similar amount of beer, tobacco, and meat, P P, for his own consumption. Three years later, however, the income which he is able to spend is diminished, for some reason or other, by one bottle of beer. Unwilling, therefore to diminish his own consumption of beer, he offers the collier, for the same amount of coal, one bottle of beer less than formerly, as shown in the parallelogram P_2 P_2. This is virtually what happened previous to the recent coal-strike. If we assume each of the articles in question to be worth 4d., we have a fall in the price of coal from 2s. per $1\frac{1}{2}$ cwt. to 1s. 8d. per $1\frac{1}{2}$ cwt., or from £1 : 7 : 6 per ton to about £1 : 2 : $2\frac{1}{2}$; but this familiar way of stating the case obscures the real point at issue. The problem for the consumer was virtually a problem connected, not with all the three fires, but with one only—with the library fire. Would the colliers take one bottle of beer for that instead of two? It is needless to say that the colliers would not wish to do so. They would not wish to lose a bottle of beer a day. But the question is, Would they be able to get the extra bottle from the consumer, if the consumer became unwilling to part with it? And the answer to this depends altogether on the result of the mental sum which is done by the consumer, not the producer—a sum

which shows him which would give him most
pleasure : one bottle of beer and a fire in his
library, or three bottles of beer which he would
have to drink in his sitting-room if he decided
not to have any fire in his library at all. The
collier, no doubt, has to do a mental sum likewise ; but it is a sum which is set for him by the
consumer, not by himself. For let us suppose
that the collier, not perceiving this, will not
submit to the reduction that the consumer
demands, and refuses to part with his coal at
less than the former price. In that case,
though his prices are kept up, his wages will
fall ; for instead of getting each day from the
consumer two chops and two cigars, and two
bottles of beer, as the price of three fires, he
will get only two chops and two cigars, without any beer at all, as the price of two fires.

Let me sum up the whole matter briefly.
In proportion as a community learns to produce and to desire an increasing number of
superfluities—that is to say, of goods not
physically necessary for the actual support of
life—it becomes more and more true with
regard to each fresh superfluity that the
amount of goods which the men who produce

it will be able to exact in exchange for it from the bulk of the community, depends on the degree of satisfaction which the bulk of the community expect to derive from it, as compared with that which they expect to derive from the other superfluities which they produce and possess themselves. If they wish to have such and such a commodity at all, there is a certain minimum that they *must* pay for it—a minimum just sufficient to keep the producer alive as a working animal; but any price that they pay for it beyond this depends altogether on the degree of value that they themselves place on it; for if the producer, in order to raise his wages, demands a larger price from them than they are naturally willing to pay, it is always open to them to say that they do not wish him to produce it at all.

This is a proposition which would be just as true of a community consisting altogether of working men, as it is of a community consisting of an employing class and an employed; and the strike-leaders, if they abolished every employer in the kingdom, would find that just as surely as at present, and far more obviously, the price of any product produced, say by any twentieth of the population, depended, not on the wages that this one-twentieth wished for, but on the prices that the other nineteen-twentieths were willing to pay.

CHAPTER IV

THE CENSUS AND THE CONDITION OF THE PEOPLE

Any reader who has grasped the simple and fundamental principles explained in the two preceding chapters—the principles by which the minimum standard of living, and the maximum wage in any given industry, are determined, and has seen how absolutely independent these are, in the last resort, of the employing classes and their profits, will be able to deal with ignorant agitators and their dupes, not as a partisan, or an agitator of another class, but as the exponent of interests common to all classes alike, and an exponent of laws which all classes must obey, or from the disregard of which all classes must suffer.

Let us now turn back from these general principles of all economic life to the general condition of the people of this country at the present moment; and consider a certain number of further facts relating to it, which bear on the specific questions most frequently touched upon by reformers. The principal sources from which the information now about to be given is derived are the several volumes of the last Census Report, and the Agricultural Returns, published by the Board of Agriculture. In order, however, to assist us in understanding them, I will refer to further information with which Mr. Giffen and other statisticians, English and Continental, have supplied us.

The various points to which I will invite the reader's attention have, as here set forth, no logical connection with one another; but they all bear on the main subject of this volume, namely, the condition of the people generally, and the means by which the truth respecting it may be best made public.

Seeing, then, that the most important of the subjects now engaging us is the manner in which wealth in this country is distributed, it will be well to convey to the reader some more or less clear idea of what the capitalised wealth possessed by this country is, or, in other words, what securities or possessions it would be found to consist of, if we were, on any day of the year, to make an analytical inventory of it.

The accompanying figure, then (Fig. 1), represents this capitalised wealth by means of a rough pictorial chart. The entire parallelogram represents the total capital value of the United Kingdom as a going concern, estimated as being something like *ten thousand million pounds sterling;* and it is divided by dark lines into thirteen compartments proportionate in size to the value of the things or goods which they represent.

It will not be necessary here to deal with the figures in detail. I propose only to call attention to a few broad facts, which are of general interest and significance, which speakers on social subjects will often find it useful to remember. We will begin, then, with considering the smallest and the two largest items represented in the chart.

The smallest item of all is money and uncoined bullion; but, small as this shows itself in the chart, in reality it is much smaller. Had it been allotted its proper proportion of space only, it would have been hardly visible to the eye. Those who are

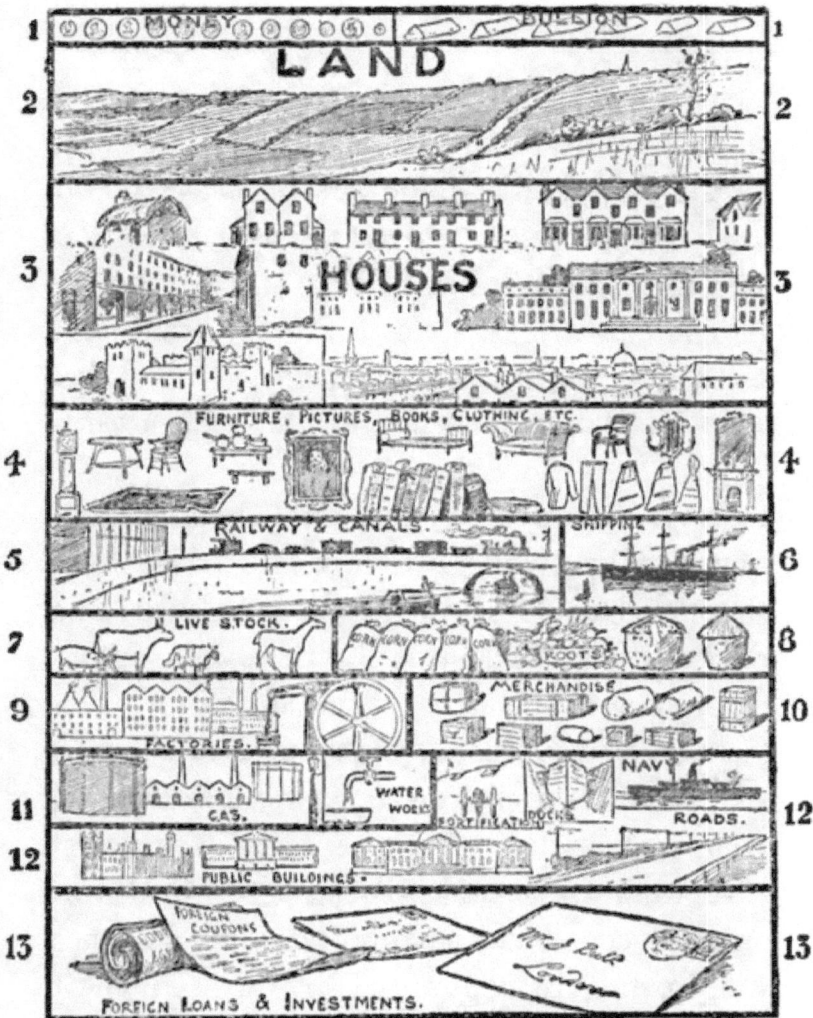

Fig. 1.

accustomed to think of wealth in terms of money, and to argue as though it were divisible and distributable like a pile of sovereigns, cannot be answered better than by an exposition of this fact.

The two largest items are houses and land, the land counting for about *fifteen hundred millions*, and the houses for *twenty-five hundred millions*.

Next comes furniture, household goods, and works of art, which are supposed to be worth about *twelve hundred millions;* and public works, imperial and local (with certain private enterprises in the shape of gas and water-works included), worth about *eight hundred millions*.

The other items, such as machinery, etc., occupy, as *capital*, so small a space as compared with their importance, because they are worn out and consumed so rapidly. For instance, iron-works are capitalised by Mr. Giffen at four years' purchase; land and railways at twenty-eight, and houses at fifteen.

But there is another fraction of our capital to which I have not yet alluded, and that is our foreign loans and investments, represented in the chart by the lowest section. These should properly come directly after the land, of which in capital value they do not fall far short; but they have been placed at the end in order to give them greater prominence: because, as related to the incomes which they represent, they offer certain points to our consideration, which, in social and political discussion, are of peculiar importance.

The income which comes into this country from abroad is in round numbers *seventy-five million pounds*, of which *twenty-one millions* comes from foreign loans, *four millions* from foreign railways, and *fifty millions* from various investments. This is a sum far greater than the entire agricultural rental of the kingdom; and the larger part of it goes ultimately in the remuneration of home labour. In other words, more than a million working-class families, representing a population of nearly five million individuals, live on wages paid to them from an income that comes to us from foreign sources. Now, with regard to this income there are two points to be noticed. One is, that it shows us how directly interested the working classes are in our possessions in other countries, and in the security of property there. The other is, that this income is made up entirely of profits and interest. Accordingly five million working-class families in the United Kingdom virtually draw their entire incomes from profits and interest; and were there any general interference with the receipt of these by the propertied and employing classes, one of the first results to the working classes of this country would be, that five millions of them would be at once deprived of the sole source from which their wages come.

Let us now pass on to the population which subsists upon all the wealth in question. This now amounts to *thirty-seven* or *thirty-eight million* persons. That fact is probably known to most people; but the general idea which this information usually conveys is a very erroneous one. It usually conveys the idea of a nation which consists principally of men and women, or—as they are often called—of citizens. The actual fact is that half the population is under the age of twenty, and nearly a third consists of children. Fig. 2 gives a general impression of what this proportion is; and for simplicity's sake the smallest body of individuals is dealt with, which will

Fig. 2

enable the smallest class to be represented by a single person—the smallest class in this case being persons over sixty-five. The reader will see, then, that out of every eighteen inhabitants, there are only eight persons, and only four males, between the ages of twenty and sixty-five. Half the population, therefore, at any given moment, may be said to be undergoing the processes of being reared and educated. Much education, however, is practical and technical, and is only gained by experience in the actual work of life. Accordingly, if we wish to consider the active population of the country, we must take into account everybody over the age of fifteen. We will now proceed to consider these; and we shall be able to realise by the aid of the opposite figure certain facts of the utmost importance in social and political discussions.

Fig. 3 contains thirty-six persons — the smallest number possible in this case to work with. Half are males and half are females. In reality, the latter exceed the former by one-fifteenth; but the difference is too small to be expressed conveniently in the illustration. Roughly speaking, bachelors bear the same

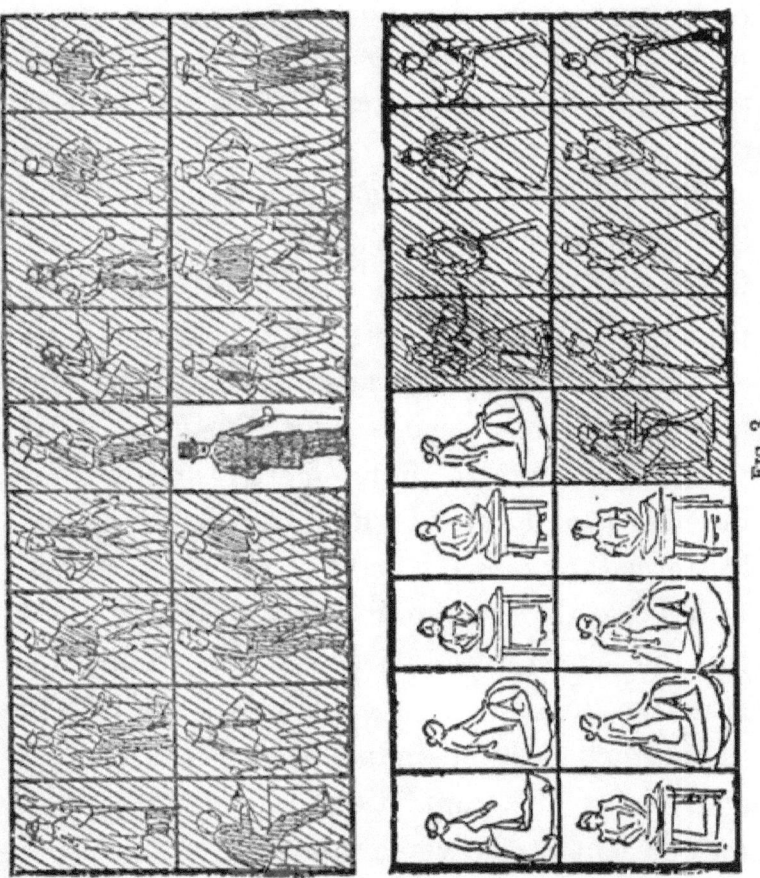

Fig. 3.

proportion to married men that spinsters bear to married women.

But the most important question which the figure illustrates is that of occupation. A vague belief prevails in the minds of many persons that there exists in this country an enormous unoccupied class of luxurious and useless persons, whose sole business it is to consume wealth in pampered and vicious idleness; and any ignorant, dishonest, or hysterical persons, turning to the Census, would be able to quote figures from it—and this has been often done—which would apparently justify this conclusion. For the unoccupied class, as enumerated in the general analysis of the population, is something like 55 per cent of the whole number.

A glance, however, at Fig. 2 will do much to explain what at first sight seems so startling; for it will at once show us that the larger part of this unoccupied class must be children. Still, when we have deducted these, we find about *nine millions* of unoccupied persons enumerated over the age of ten—*one million seven hundred thousand* males, and *seven and a half million* females. Even these reduced numbers are at first sight somewhat staggering: but at all events we see that the larger portion of the unoccupied consists of women. We will consider these first.

If we deduct all females under the age of fifteen, the unoccupied women will be reduced to a number about equal to half the entire number of females above the age of fifteen. Now of these females above the age of fifteen, more than half are married; therefore the number of unoccupied women in this country is less than the number of married women. Speaking broadly, the mass of women in this country, who are returned in the Census Report as unoccupied, are married women; whilst a fraction of these even is returned as occupied. The position of affairs is indicated with substantial accuracy in Fig. 3. The shaded portions of that figure represent the occupied population, the unshaded portion the unoccupied; and of the women returned as unoccupied most are married. I say "returned as unoccupied"; for are they so in reality? They are very far from being so, as was pointed out by the compilers of the previous Census. The bulk of them are engaged in occupations second in importance to none—the occupation of looking after the home welfare of their husbands—and one more momentous yet — the occupation of feeding the infancy and forming the character in childhood of that great third of our population who will so soon be in their parents' places.

And now let us turn to the men. Of the *one million seven hundred thousand* occupied males, over ten years of age, about *one million two hundred thousand* are under fifteen, and about *two hundred and fifty thousand* are under twenty or over sixty-five, so that of males between twenty and sixty-five there are not more than *two hundred and fifty thousand* unoccupied; and this number includes something like fifty thousand of the insane, and the unoccupied blind and deaf and dumb males between the ages in question. If we deduct these, we reduce the number of the unoccupied to two hundred thousand; and again, of those two hundred thousand, more than forty thousand are men who have retired from business after their fifty-fifth year, and nearly six thousand are pensioners above the same age; whilst the number of males between twenty and sixty-five returned as "living on their own means" is not more than ninety-two thousand. If, therefore, we estimate the unoccupied males capable under pressure of being added to the army of the occupied, as numbering as many as a hundred and fifty thousand, we shall be far beyond the mark rather than short of it. The result, then, on the entire community of the unoccupied giving themselves to industry would be to shorten the toil of the occupied classes by about one minute in the hour. Accordingly, so far as it relates to the unoccupied males, Fig. 3 must be corrected. That shows one unoccupied adult male to seventeen occupied. There is in reality only one to sixty.

We will now pass to a question which, more perhaps than any other, throws a distinct light on the welfare of the great mass of the people, namely, the question of how they are lodged. The Census with regard to this gives us an amount of information, the existence of which is probably unsuspected by many.

The Census divides the houses or tenements occupied by separate families in England and Wales into two broad classes—those which consist of five rooms and upwards, and those which consist of less than five rooms. About half the tenements belong to the latter class. That is to say, about half the families in England and Wales occupy tenements containing four rooms, and under; and these are classified into tenements of four rooms, three rooms, two rooms, and one room. What proportion of the families in question occupy each? The proportion can be understood instantly by reference to Fig. 4. It will there be seen that out of every fifty tenements twenty-three consist of four rooms, twelve of three, eleven of two, and only four of one. In many of the two-roomed tenements, however, there is a considerable amount of overcrowding—the term "overcrowding" being used by the compilers of the Census as meaning an average of more than two persons to one room. But the proportion of the population thus lodged is not more than 11 per cent; and in many cases, as will be pointed out presently, such overcrowding is not by any means an indication of extreme poverty.

The most important question, however, for us to consider is not how the population are lodged now, but whether, under the existing economic system, their condition is tending to

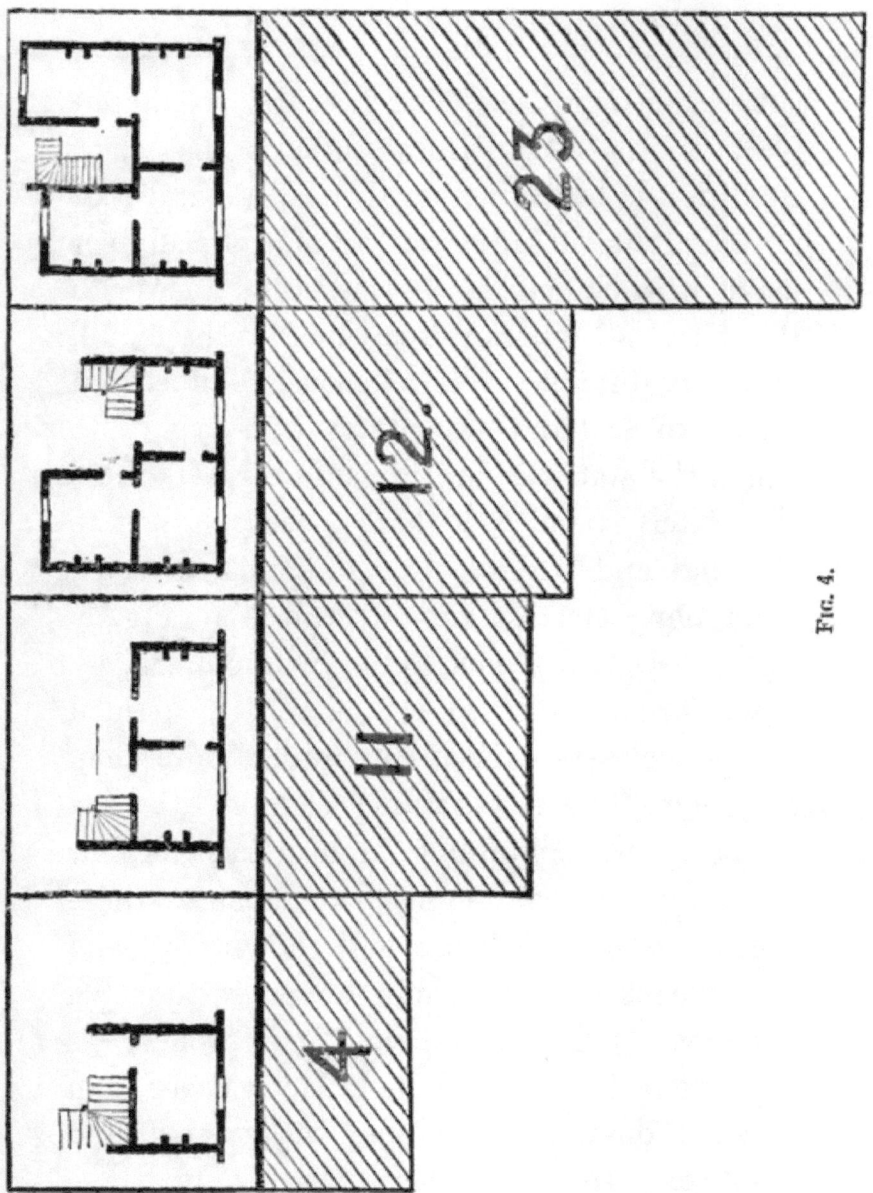

Fig. 4.

get better or worse. The favourite commonplace of the socialistic agitator is that their condition is becoming steadily worse, and that nothing but an industrial revolution can ever make it grow better. A conclusive answer to this false and ignorant doctrine is to be found, put very briefly, in the Census volume that relates to Scotland—a country with regard to which the statistics are in some respects more elaborately tabulated than those relating to England and Wales. The statistics to which I am now referring are illustrated in Fig. 5. The houses and tenements in Scotland can, by the information given us, be readily divided into six classes—those containing more than ten rooms, those containing from five to ten rooms, those containing from three to four rooms, those containing two rooms, those consisting of one room with a window, and those consisting of one room without a window. Of this last and miserable class there were in Scotland in 1881 no fewer than seven thousand, containing seven thousand families. In 1891 there were only three hundred and ninety-eight, of which only eight were in towns, the remainder being probably

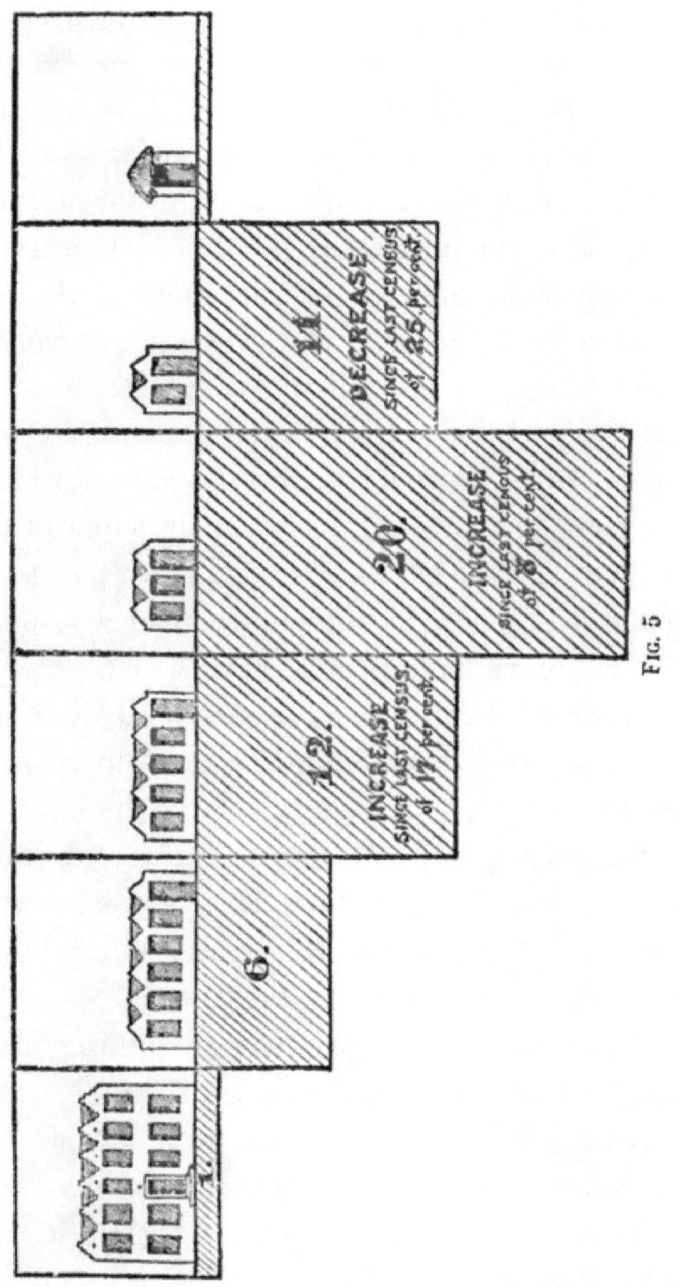

Fig. 5

remote Highland cabins. Of the remaining five classes of dwelling, Fig. 5 shows the numbers, out of every fifty families, occupying each. But the important point to notice is not the numbers themselves, but their respective increase or decrease. If we confine ourselves to dwellings of less than five rooms, we see that the poorer dwellings are decreasing in proportion to their poverty, and the superior class increasing in proportion to their superiority. The windowless cabins, as we have seen, have almost disappeared; the one-roomed dwellings with windows have decreased 25 per cent; the two-roomed dwellings have increased by 8 per cent, and the three-roomed and four-roomed dwellings by 17 per cent. It would be hard to discover a sign of general progress more definite and distinct than this, or one which a speaker could use with greater effect when explaining to a popular audience the real nature of the economic changes that are taking place round us in the natural course of things.

And now let us turn back from Scotland to the country considered generally, and examine a different set of facts, also recorded in the Census, which will throw further light on the condition and progress of the community. It will be found that they illustrate and corroborate those that have been already mentioned, and are equally adapted for use by political speakers.

In Fig. 6 the numerals on the circumference indicate the percentage of increase or decrease in each of the industries, trades, or professions named, between the years 1881 and 1891. The shaded portion represents the growth of the population during the same period. The reader will therefore be able to see at once, not only whether any body of men has increased or decreased absolutely, but also whether it has increased or decreased relatively to the total population. It will be seen, for instance, that the clergy of the Established Church have increased absolutely by 11 per cent, but that relatively to the population they have not increased, they have only kept pace with it. The Nonconformist clergy, on the other hand, though they have absolutely increased by 3 per cent, have relatively to the population decreased by 8 per cent; whilst the Roman Catholic clergy have increased absolutely by 20 per cent, and relatively to the population by 9 per cent.

To keep, however, to questions of merely economic interest, the only large industrial class that has decreased to any serious extent absolutely is the agricultural labourers. To the question of agriculture I shall refer again presently. I will only observe here that the number of farmers is nearly the same as it was in 1881, whilst the number of market gardeners has increased by 20 per cent, and there is also an immense increase in the amount of land used for market gardening.

The great cotton industry, as will be seen, has kept pace with the population. But the principal facts to which I wish to call attention are of a more general character than these. They are facts which indicate that whilst, during the period dealt with by the Census, the wealthier classes have not greatly changed their position relatively to the community, there has been a great growth of wealth amongst the people generally, and an immense accession to the ranks of the lower middle classes.

With regard to the wealthier classes it is

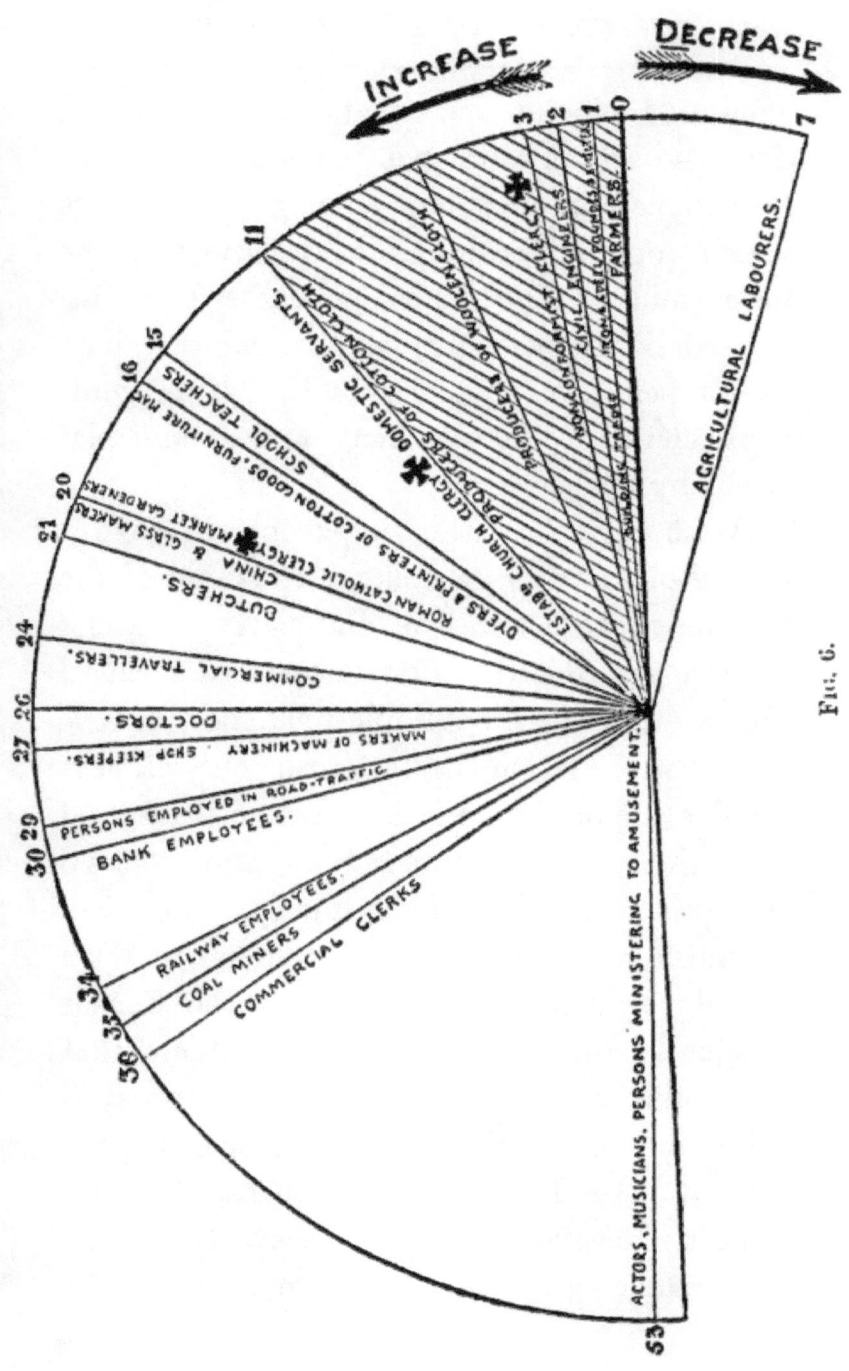

Fig. 6.

enough to point out that the number of domestic servants has not increased relatively to the population; but amongst the classes which, roughly speaking, are described as the lower-middle, the school teachers have increased by 15 per cent, commercial travellers by 24 per cent, shopkeepers by 27 per cent, bank clerks by 30 per cent, and commercial clerks by 34 per cent.

With regard to the shopkeepers I have a special observation to make. It is one of the fundamental doctrines of the party of social agitation—a doctrine first formulated by Karl Marx—that the inevitable tendency of the capitalistic system is to crush out all the smaller productive and distributive firms, and mass their business into a number of colossal enterprises, which will constantly increase in magnitude and decrease in number. With regard to distributive enterprise the Census absolutely refutes this view, and shows that the number of distributive enterprises is increasing more than twice as fast as the population. The Census returns, in this respect, however, contain a certain amount of possible error, as the compilers of the report indicate. I have therefore had recourse to the London Post-office Directory for the years 1881 and 1891, and compared the number of separate businesses in London— productive and distributive — at the two periods; and I find that the actual number of separate businesses has increased by more than 11 per cent, whilst, if we consider the number of partners whose names appear in these businesses, the increase has been 20 per cent. Thus, from whatever point we look at the matter, the smaller businesses, instead of being crushed out, are increasing more rapidly than the population.

And now let us consider the great masses of the people. There are four facts illustrated in Fig. 6 which throw light upon this. There is the increase of 15 per cent in the school teachers, which shows the progress of education; there is an increase of 21 per cent in the butchers, which shows the general increase of meat consumption; there is an increase of 26 per cent in the doctors, which shows the growing attention given to the popular health; and, lastly, there is an increase of 53 per cent in the persons who professionally minister to amusement. It may be said that a part of this increase is an increase in actors, singers and others, who amuse the wealthier classes. This is true; but the figures of the Census show us that the increase in this class is comparatively small, and that the great increase has taken place amongst showmen, tumblers, clowns, and so forth—that is to say, in that precise section which ministers exclusively to the amusement of the poorer classes. The increase in this section is not less than 80 per cent. Thus the masses have become able in ten years very nearly to double their expenditure on amusement. Let me add to these facts another, not indicated in the diagram. The computed capital of the Post-office Savings Banks for England and Wales was in 1881 £33,771,412. In 1891 it was £66,018,228. That is to say, in ten years it had very nearly doubled itself.

Of the various points that have just been mentioned, there now remain three about which it would be well to speak more particularly, as each one of these is constantly made the subject of loose and ignorant rhetoric. The first of these is the position of the principal religious bodies in the kingdom, on which turns the great question of disestablishment; the second is the condition of agriculture in this country, as compared with its condition in others; and the third is the question of the housing of the working classes, regarded in connection with facts which have not yet been mentioned.

Let us begin with the question of religion, which can be dealt with very briefly. It is deeply to be regretted that a proper religious Census has never yet been permitted. But though we cannot directly tell the respective numbers of those belonging to different denominations, we can get some indication of the truth from the number of the religious ministers. This the Census gives us; and the results can be seen at a glance in Fig. 7. In this, as in former cases, the number dealt with in the diagram is the smallest which it is possible to work with for the purpose required. It will be seen, then, from Fig. 7, that of every nineteen ministers of religion in England and Wales thirteen are clergymen of the Established Church, five are ministers of various Nonconformist bodies, and one is a Roman Catholic priest.

FIG. 7.

Let us now go back to agriculture—the only industry in this country which has shown symptoms of continuous decline. It is no part of the purpose of this volume to set forth any views as to the future of British agriculture. All that I shall attempt to do here is to call the reader's attention to a number of facts which are not generally appreciated or even known, and which will assist the reader in forming his own conclusions. They are facts some of which are susceptible of various interpretations; but there are certain popular fallacies which they at once refute; so there is one undoubted moral which may at all events be drawn from them.

Radical and Socialistic reformers are constantly declaring that agriculture in this country would revive if we did but change our land-system, and committed the cultivation of the soil to small cultivators, who either actually owned the areas cultivated by them, or held them in perpetuity from the State on payment of a land-tax. Indeed a "labour member" in the House of Commons actually said, during the last Parliament, that were the land thus cultivated it would yield four times what it does at present.

Let any one who is inclined to believe in this demented rhetoric turn to Fig. 8. It illustrates three orders of facts connected with contemporary agriculture; and will, amongst other things, enable the reader to compare the productivity of the soil, as cultivated in this country, with its productivity in countries such as France, Sweden, or Austria, where the very conditions demanded by our own agitators already prevail largely; France having more than a million landowners, with an average holding of thirteen acres, whilst 33 per cent of the soil of the Austrian Empire, and more than half the soil of Sweden, is held by peasants. The comparison is not complete, as its basis is the production of wheat only; but it is nevertheless valuable.

The upper series of parallelograms in Fig. 8, marked W W, and decreasing like steps, represents the number of bushels of wheat per acre yielded by the countries named. Of all the countries named, except Holland, the yield in this country is the highest. It is some 80 per cent higher than that of France, with its peasant proprietors, and some 250 per cent higher than that of America. The actual yield per acre, however, is not the only point to be considered. We must also take into account the immediate labour expended in producing

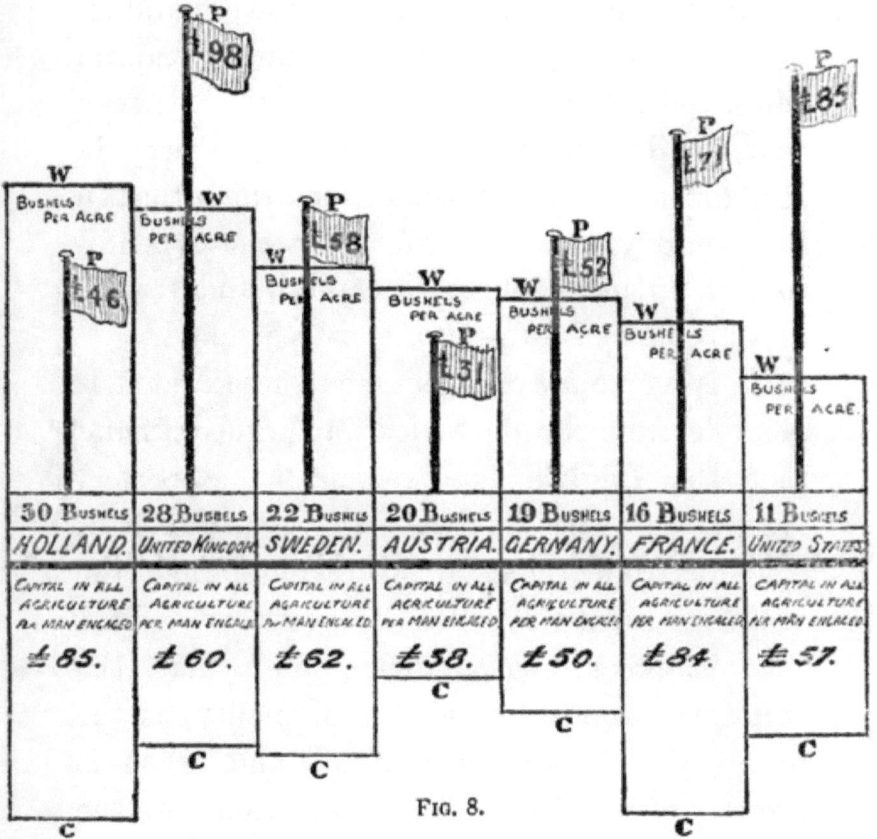

Fig. 8.

this, and the amount of capital by which that labour is assisted. And, taking these into consideration, the agricultural system of this kingdom is seen to be, acre for acre, the most efficient in the civilised world. The flags P P indicate, by the sums marked on them, the value of the agricultural produce per hand engaged in agriculture; and the lower parallelograms, C C, represent the amount of capital employed for each hand. It will thus be seen that, whilst the yield of wheat per acre in Holland is but 6 per cent more than that in this country, this excess involves the expenditure of 40 per cent more capital, and results in a product of 50 per cent less per hand.

It is by no means insinuated here that it is possible, from the above *data*, to argue off hand that the English land-system is a perfect system, or even the best existing; but it is evident from them, at all events, that the ordinary attacks levelled by agitators against the system are groundless; and that the agitators' promises of a reign of plenty, as the result of "drastic legislation," and what is grotesquely called "the restoration of the people to the land," or of "the land to the people," is a falsehood, without the smallest warrant in experience. It is quite conceivable that agriculture may be revived in time by the application of the genius of gifted individuals—of men of science and men of enterprise—to farming. Much may be done by technical improvements; nothing can be done by revolution.

And now we come to the last subject which will be discussed in this volume, namely, the housing of the working classes. We have already considered the actual condition of these classes in this respect as an indication of their condition generally. Let us consider it once more, in order to realise the nature of the problem presented to us by the miserable and demoralising dwellings occupied by a section of the population.

According to the ordinary agitator the cause of this misery is simple, and so also is its remedy. The cause of it is the landlord; and the remedy for it is to rob him or get rid of him. To whatever conclusion an examination of facts may bring us, it will at all events free us from the dominion of this popular fallacy. Here and there a population may be housed miserably owing to the extortions of a bad landlord; but the connection between high rents and insufficient accommodation is a mere local or temporary accident, as will be shown presently by a set of very curious statistics relating to the housing of the poor classes in seventeen of the most important towns in the kingdom. But before passing to the consideration of these, let us pause for a moment to examine a question of fact, which is constantly and wantonly misrepresented by the rancour of uneducated, and even of educated, agitators. I refer to the rental of the country taken as a whole, including the rental of the ground occupied by houses. How agitators arrive at their figures is in some cases very difficult to say; but there has been recently an agreement between most of our more violent reformers to estimate the rental of this country, agricultural and urban, apart from the rent paid for the actual structure of the houses, at a *hundred and sixty million pounds*[1] annually. A sillier and more monstrous exaggeration it is not possible to conceive. The real facts of the case—speaking broadly—are accessible with extreme ease; and there is no excuse for those who persist

---

[1] See, for instance, *The Villager's Magna Charta*, by J. M. Davidson, Barrister-at-law, p. 15.

in misrepresenting them. Any one who is familiar with the pages of "The Statistical Abstract" knows where to find that the agricultural rental of the United Kingdom is about *fifty-six million pounds*, and that the house rental is a *hundred and forty-four millions*. The only point here which presents any semblance of difficulty is one presented by this latter sum: for it includes not only the rental of the houses, but that of the ground on which they are built. How are we to discover what portion of it is paid for the ground? It so happens that there is a rough and ready way of discovering, not indeed what is the exact fraction paid for the ground, but the maximum amount that could, under existing circumstances, be conceivably paid for it. The most recent investigations into the actual ground rental of London, which was undertaken under the auspices of the London County Council, have resulted in the conclusion that the gross rental of the metropolis was about *forty million pounds*, and the actual ground rental about *fifteen millions*. This, however, is an extreme estimate, most statisticians estimating the ground rental at thirteen millions. For argument's sake, however, let us assume it to be fifteen millions. Now of all towns in the kingdom the gross rental per head is highest in London, the reason being the superior value of the land. According to Mr. Mulhall the rental per head in London is as compared with the rental per head in Brighton as one hundred and fifty is to one hundred and ten; with the rental per head in Newcastle as one hundred and fifty is to one hundred and three; with that in Liverpool and Manchester as one hundred and fifty is to one hundred; with that in Birmingham and Bristol as one hundred and fifty is to eighty: and as regards the other towns in the kingdom, the proportion of the gross rental which is ground rent is in London more than double the average. Let us, then, for argument's sake, make the extreme supposition that the proportion borne by ground rental to gross rental in London obtains throughout all the towns in the kingdom—that is to say, that out of every £40 of gross rental £15 is ground rent. Now the entire house rental of the kingdom being a *hundred and forty-four millions*, we shall, on the above assumption, get at the entire ground rent by this simple proportion sum—as forty is to fifteen so is one hundred and forty-four to the rent in question. The answer will be about *fifty-four million* pounds. This, added to the agricultural rental of *fifty-six millions*, gives a total rental of a *hundred and ten millions*, instead of a *hundred and sixty;* and even so high a figure as this can be reached only by the absurd imputation to every country town in the kingdom of a ground rental which is per acre nearly double that of Bristol and Birmingham. Putting aside the exaggeration involved in the above calculation, it will be found impossible to estimate the rental of the soil of this country—building land included—at more than a *hundred millions* annually. The additional *sixty millions* which figure in the computations of the land reformers are therefore an entire invention of their own: and whatever plausibility there may be in their theory that the worst of the evils connected with the present housing of the poor are due to the extortions of the ground landlord, depends on their imputing to these landlords an annual abstraction from the public of *sixty million* pounds, which is altogether imaginary.

And now let us turn from these general facts to the facts already alluded to, connected with seventeen of the most important towns of the kingdom. Of these towns special mention is made in the Census Report with reference to the question of overcrowding. The meaning attached to the term *overcrowding* is in each case the same, namely, the occupation of one room as a dwelling by more than two persons; and the percentage of the population that is overcrowded is given in each case. The facts thus brought to light are illustrated in Fig. 9.

The parallelogram of which the figure consists is divided into seventeen horizontal sections, each section representing the population of a town. The *shaded* portions of each represent that portion of the population in question which is housed more or less satisfactorily. The *unshaded* portions represent the percentage which is in each case overcrowded. It will be seen that this percentage is highest in certain northern towns, and in Plymouth; the percentage of overcrowding in

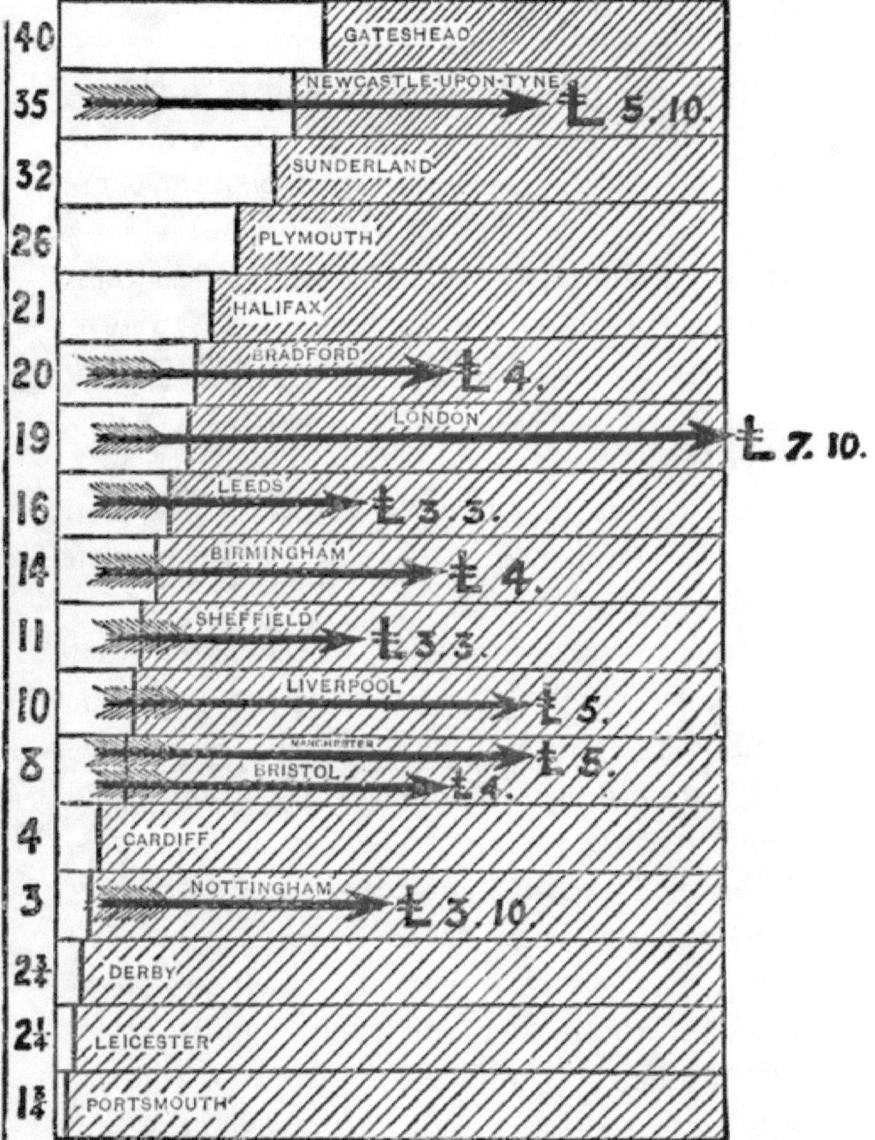

Fig. 9.

London being not half of what it is in Gateshead, and not much more than half of what it is in Newcastle. Again, in Liverpool the overcrowding is about half of what it is in London; whilst in Manchester and Bristol it is less than a half, in Preston less than a quarter, and in Nottingham less than a sixth. Again, Plymouth and Portsmouth are towns in many ways of the same character; and yet Plymouth is one of the four most overcrowded towns in the kingdom, whilst there is in Portsmouth hardly any overcrowding at all.

If there were any truth in the theory that overcrowding is due to the extortion of the landlords, we should find that the percentage of overcrowding in the towns just named had some general correspondence with the rents. I have, therefore, indicated by the black arrows in the diagram the rental per head in those of the towns named, which are mentioned in the most recent tables published by Mr. Mulhall. The result of collating the two sets of facts—those referring to overcrowding and those referring to rent—is singular. Even so shrewd an observer as Mr. Charles Booth is disposed to think that rent will explain many seeming anomalies; but it evidently supplies us with the general solution of the problem whatsoever. Between high rents and overcrowding there is obviously no connection, except here and there accidental ones. For though Newcastle rents are the second highest in the kingdom, and though Newcastle stands second amongst our overcrowded towns, the highest rents of all are those of London; and in point of overcrowding London stands seventh. Again, in Sheffield the overcrowding is greater than it is in Liverpool, and yet rent in Sheffield is 40 per cent less.

Since I first drew public attention to these facts, I have received letters from various parts of the kingdom, mentioning a variety of local circumstances that may explain them, such as the inherited habits of the people in this and that district, the architectural history of this and that town, and the nature of the ground on which it is built. For instance, it has been pointed out that overcrowding in Plymouth, as estimated by the number of families occupying single rooms, is due, in part at all events, to the fact that the houses now occupied by a section of the labouring classes were built for a wealthier class originally, and that the rooms in them were exceptionally spacious; whilst much of the overcrowding in Newcastle is said to be due to the peculiar lie of the ground, which limits the number of houses capable of being built in the immediate neighbourhood of the river, the locality most convenient for a large proportion of the working classes.

This is not the place for pursuing these questions of detail farther; but the facts already mentioned point unmistakably to one great conclusion—that overcrowding is an accident of our industrial system, not a necessary accompaniment of it. The same industrial system prevails in Derby and Leicester that prevails at Gateshead and in London, and yet Fig. 9 will show us how small the overcrowding in the two former towns is. Conditions which can be procured in one place can probably, with time, and care, and prudence, be procured in all.

And the moral to be drawn from these facts as to the housing of the poor is equally applicable to all the problems which a progressive civilisation presents to the consideration of the reformer. There are always social questions;

but there neither is, nor ever can be, any social question. Every reform is a question of detail —of careful and circumstantial modification. It is not a question of revolutionising fundamental principles : and though nearly all general statements are true only when allowance is made for many exceptions, the following general statement is almost universal in its truth—that should a man wish to identify the points in the social system which are unalterable, he will find them in the very points which Socialists and similar reformers most desire to alter.

THE END

www.ingramcontent.com/pod-product-compliance
Lightning Source LLC
Chambersburg PA
CBHW030320170426
43202CB00009B/1080